"Funny how fallin' feels like flyin'…for a little while."

Song Lyrics by Colin Farrell and Jeff Bridges

This book looks at a few causes of falling societies. It was written during a time when most were still saying "Wheee…"

"Don't skate to where the puck is. Skate to where the puck is _going_."

Wayne Gretzky

FARMING HUMANS

Written between 2018, and May 2020 with editing and corrections throughout the remainder of 2020

Author: Larry Elford

Publisher: Visual Investigations

Contact: Visualinvestigations@shaw.ca

Printed in the USA

V13 Sept 2020

Project: Book 2
282 pages
72, 876 words
107 Megabytes

ISBN: 9798643881599   Farming Humans

Non-Fiction

Introduction

FARMING HUMANS
A "How To" Guide for Dictators and Dummies

How the well connected can capture and exploit the economic efforts of humanity.

As I began this an estimated 41.4 percent of the total U.S. population — 135 million people — were either poor or low-income while 500,000 are homeless. Three men own as much wealth as the bottom half of American society owns.

"Do the rich and powerful, have secret back-door access into the system for themselves, at the expense of everyone else?" The answer is yes and this book shows how.

The U.S. abolished slavery in 1865 with the 13th Amendment to the U.S. Constitution.

Farming Humans is about modern day methods of treating persons unfairly, or creating secret advantages for "some persons", but not for others. Not methods based upon skin color as in the past, but upon manipulation of political, economic and legal power. It occurs when power is dispensed selectively, or used in a self-serving or corrupt manner.

Some might call it a form of economic bondage. One where vulnerable people are more likely to be economic slaves, while still believing they are free. My hope is to reveal how those unfairly rigged principles of poverty were silently put into place for millions of unsuspecting people.

One definition of corruption is "the abuse of public power or authority, for private gains."

Unfair systems have been intentionally created to elevate some humans over others, and above the "the natural laws of poverty", into the arms of prosperity. These are a few of those corrupt tricks.

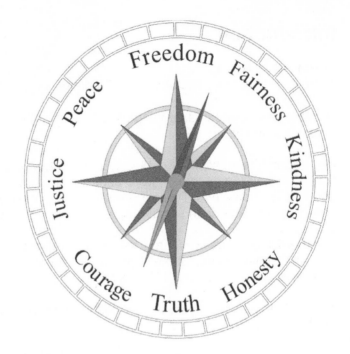

Dedications

This book is dedicated to your grandchildren and mine. We leave them this world, and my hope is that we also leave them with the opportunities, freedoms and fairness that we once enjoyed.

With thanks to Jane Jacobs, now deceased, and her 2006 book "Dark Age Ahead". In this concise work, she described a decline in social and professional standards which could bring a "dark age" upon society.

That and Agnotology.

Agnotology: The study of willful acts to spread confusion and deceit, often to unduly influence the public in order to sell a product, or win political or other favor.

https://www.bbc.com/future/article/20160105-the-man-who-studies-the-spread-of-ignorance?fbclid=IwAR2j_7vZc4OJq8-q7xM5r-UBQNW8GPCJXSdKrweBx4UWVpQLwCuQuxZBHqbl

"The study of money, above all other fields in economics, is one in which complexity is used to disguise truth or to evade truth, not to reveal it." -John Kenneth Galbraith

With gratitude to the following for their counsel, guidance and help in the creation of this book, and those who suffered through very rough drafts in its creation:

Les Elford
Norman Elford
Dennis Kamitomo
Leslie Whitlow
Patricia Buswell
Joe Killoran
Tina Brown

I believe freedom only exists in a fair and just society.

I also believe that:
Freedom requires Fairness.
Fairness requires Kindness.
Kindness involves Honesty.
Honesty involves Truth.
Truth requires Courage.
Courage enables Justice.
Justice allows Peace.
Peace allows Freedom.

Those are some values I try to remind myself of. In a world where right and wrong is easily confused and reversed, it is imperative to seek principles to try and live by.
-- Larry Elford 2019

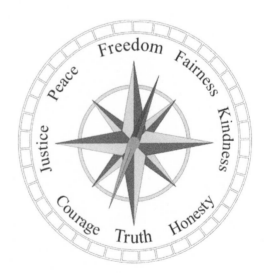

This book is written in three parts to show a general (but imperfect) timeline of events.

1. **Yesterday   (Causes)**

2. **Today   (Effects)**

3. **Tomorrow   (Solutions)**

CONTENTS

1. **Yesterday   (Causes)**

2. Today_____(Effects)

3. Tomorrow __(Solutions)

Chapter 1   375 BC
The Ring Of Gyges

<u>This Chapter is about:</u> A 2400 year old thought experiment about how powers of invisibility would cause any man to commit crime. The ability to invisibly commit crime is the #1 Trick for Farming Humans.

<u>It is important because:</u> It is important for society to learn of hidden or taboo topics such as organized crime by professionals and public servants. This 2400 year old crime story is still at work in 2020, making our society very fragile.

Around the year 375 BC, The Greek philosopher Plato wrote a dialogue called "The Republic", concerning honesty and justice in men and governance systems. Within this work is a legend of a magic ring, called the Ring of Gyges, which is a mythical magical artifact which granted its owner the power to become invisible at will.

The story was used to illustrate a thought experiment by Plato which concluded that absolute power corrupts absolutely. It is relevant today, as this book touches upon examples where social constructs grant powers like those granted by the Ring of Gyges.

Plato argues that the powers of the Ring of Gyges, invisibility and anonymity, is the only barrier between a just and an unjust person. He argues that we would all be unjust if we had a cloak of anonymity. Injustice is far more profitable. Humans are only 'just', when necessary.

How to get away with almost any crime, and not be put in jail is a power owned by the modern corporation, 2400 years later. What if humans today are following belief systems created in a time when not more than a handful of people imagined the consequences, and which grant magical-like powers over humans?

> "If a man could obtain the Ring of Gyges and make himself invisible, there is no wealth on earth that he would not take."
> Plato in Book 2 of "The Republic" 360 BCE

In 2017, I told this Ring of Gyges story in the parliamentary press gallery in Ottawa, Canada. I was there to shine light into dark corners of corrupt systems of investment and finance. Financial, regulatory and legal systems have co-operated to create perfect invisibility for activities which I knew from working on the inside, to be crimes and coverups by professionals.

It is important for society to learn of hidden or taboo topics such as organized crime. Also of the psychological trap of double-binds, which make it forbidden to reveal abuses or organized crimes by powerful men and systems.

Double binds are used to gain control over others. They occur in daily life and also in extreme abuse. Victims often feel confusion, rage, and despair at their entrapment and apparent lack of options.

A double bind is technically defined as a situation where:
1. If you do some Action, you'll be punished
2. If you don't do that Action, you'll also be punished
3. If you bring up the unfairness, you'll be punished
4. You can't leave the situation
See also "Whistleblower" topic.

Farming Humans becomes easy when taboo subjects (things that no one is allowed to talk about) become the very things that powerful abusers use to get ahead.

TABOO: Taboo is something society considers a no-no. For example, it is taboo to ask people how much money they earn, or how ethically they earn it.

When we say that certain subjects are "taboo," it means they are off-limits for discussion. For example, many abusive practices have been "taboo" topics when powerful or important persons are involved. They occur, but are not freely discussed in public.

This Story Begins 2400 Years Ago

<u>This is about:</u> The 2400 year old story of giving people immunity from being honest or just.

<u>It is important because:</u> Today, we grant the greatest crimes in society, immunity or invisibility from being prosecuted. A legend from Plato helps to better understand crimes draining society today.

I held a press conference in the Parliamentary Press Gallery in Ottawa, Canada on June 7, 2017.

I was in Ottawa to provide expert testimony to a Parliamentary Finance Committee. It was the fourth legislative committee that I have been fortunate enough to testify in on a topic of systemic financial crime.

I was invited after news stories by our National broadcast agency revealed patterns of employee and public abuse by the banking industry. The news had shown that several thousand Canadian bank employees had contacted CBC News Go Public's Erica Johnson and Enza Uda, and told them of being pressured by employers to do financially harmful things to the bank's customers. (The Double Bind of "sell this product (even at harm to clients)...or lose your job")

It was making some employees sick, with the pressure and job requirement to financially assault the people they were supposed to serve. I knew how they felt. I too, was a former bank employee who witnessed that the way to get ahead in the bank, was to be the bank-product salesman who harvested clients the hardest... financially speaking. Every day management compared product-sales employees (then fraudulently termed "advisors") with the top performing salespersons in the firm. This raised the bar to where the bank seemed satisfied only with those sociopathic enough to measure up to the top sales performers, an impossible task for those who were not willing to financially harm their customers.

It was a psychological "double-bind" where the person caught in it, is forced to make a choice between two options, both of which end badly for the chooser. Do you keep your job by harming customers, or do you serve clients honestly and lose your job?
The banks were milking a 20th Century reputation of trust and integrity, to harm and harvest their customers in a ruthless manner. The public had not yet caught on to the new "Counterparty risk" of "misplaced trust in financial institutions". Most Canadians believed that their once-trusted banks were dealing with the public like just they did in the 1980's or 1990's, which was a totally different world.

Thus my presentation to the Parliamentary press was based on an ethics lesson from 2400 years earlier.

I presented the following statement (in italics) to the press conference in Ottawa:

I believe this issue is important, in that systemic financial crime by financial institutions, costs Canada as much as the cost of all criminal acts in the land…combined.

The Ring of Gyges is a mythical magical artifact mentioned by the philosopher Plato in Book Two of his Republic.

It granted its owner the power to become invisible at will. Through the story of the ring, Republic considers whether an intelligent person would be moral if he did not have to fear being caught and punished for doing injustices.

I mention the legend of the Ring of Gyges at this time because to me it explains how North American Financial systems can utilize regulatory tricks and regulatory capture to invoke powers similar to the Ring of Gyges. The power to get away with anything you can imagine, and to never be discovered, or held to account.

This legend reminds me of how the financial system is now above our system of laws, and seems able to get away with not being held to account, for harm they do, including intentional harm to the country and to Canadians.

I am in Ottawa to make a presentation to the Standing Committee on Finance that is looking into Canadian banks and financial players, and at how they treat their clients and employees behind the curtains.

I gained my experience by working for two decades within some of the largest financial institutions in Canada. I worked in the investment industry through the 1990's when 90% of the investment business in the country was acquired by five banks.

The experience that changed my life was when I placed an article in my local newspaper that showed investors how to buy mutual funds without having to pay any commissions or loads.

What I struggled with, and spent time debating with my manager at the time, before publishing, was whether it was beneficial to let the public know that they did not have to pay fees…or to keep the public in silence.

Later I learned that the bank investment holdings for clients contained $2 billion dollars worth of mutual fund investments. These were sold to clients by salespersons on a commission. Fully 71% of all those funds were sold utilizing the 'highest compensation" choice available to the salesperson, (the 'deferred sales charge' or DSC) and the one which penalized the client the most to pay this hidden commission.

When I ran an article in my local newspaper telling investors how they could purchase mutual funds without paying any commissions it was a hit, but not in a good way…..I found out much later that despite mutual fund pricing having been de-regulated in 1987, that not a single example could be found where the public was made aware that these investment fees were de-regulated and that all fees were negotiable.

The bank I worked for simply made the decision to <u>never</u> allow this information to be revealed to the public.

Clients were, and still to this day, also kept in the dark about the salesperson licenses. Most Canadians are surreptitiously given a salesperson when they ask for a financial professional….it is the greatest unprotected bait-and-switch game in Canada and it costs

Canadians as much as the cost of all criminal acts in the land, as measured by the national crime statistics of the government.

Unfortunately, there are no government or other agencies in Canada which compile a list of financial harms done by our most trusted financial institutions. Just as the 2000 year old legend would suggest, however, we find that some sectors of our society appear to be well above the reach of our laws.

Back to the sale of Deferred Sales Charge mutuals, when identical funds were available which were cheaper, better investments for clients, but did not have the 5% commission kick to the dealer and the salesperson to share.

When I informed my clients and the public that they could purchase these funds more cheaply than most salespeople would allow, I believed I was doing the company a favor by doing my investment clients a favor. I believed that was my job. You see I was a much younger man and I had yet to learn that there are often two games going on in the financial industry, the game that the industry would like the public to see, and the hidden, not for public knowledge game.

To make a long story short, when my financial institution was forced to choose between following industry rules of fairness, honesty and good faith, or of taking the path that made them the most money, they chose to go for the money, and eliminate, anyone or anything that got in the way of those higher revenues, even if it meant doing intentional harm to the investment clients of the firm.

No amount of discussion or debate about the bank's principles, codes of ethics, nor rules of honesty could sway managers, and I was threatened with being fired if I ever made such an error again.

Mutual fund fees were deregulated in 1987, and here it was the year 2000, and the bank was still hiding from investment customers the best and most effective investment advice from its clients, in order to earn more commissions.

The 5% DSC commission was worth $100 million dollars in commissions paid to the bank on the $2 billion of holdings.

I managed over $100 million dollars at RBC at this time, and did my best to place the interests of my clients first, and I ran into a brick wall with this discussion. There are many other stories like that, of double dipping, or churning funds, of selling house-brand funds, to todays most common practice of fee based "advisor" accounts where the client does not even get the services of a registered "advisor", much less a true fiduciary "adviser".

It was not until 2013, about a decade after leaving the investment industry, and almost 3 decades after I entered, that I learned what brings me here today…myself, working with the Small Investor Protection Association received the startling news after decades or mystery, that Securities regulators did not consider the "title" of "advisor", spelled using "or" at the end, to mean the same thing as the word "adviser" spelled "er", as it is found in the law. Could a simple 'vowel movement' be used to fool ten million Canadian investors into trusting the non-registered, non-fiduciary salesperson?

This seemed too ridiculous to even consider, so we let it go until written confirmation was received from the Canadian Securities Administrators and a few of the 13 Canadian Securities Commissions. Not until we had their confirmation did we believe it. The deception of Canadians was not an accident, but a clever ploy to deceive. To deceive them to make it easier to avail themselves of the rightful returns of the investor. The deception allowed brokers to overcharge clients or to take advantage of them in other meaningful ways. Ways that were sufficient to cut the retirement security of many Canadians by half or more.

Cutting, skimming or harvesting Canadians financial security by 50% to 60% using deception and trickery is certainly illegal, and VERY profitable. What does the industry do? It hides the illegal acts, 'shoots the messenger', by pressuring anyone who tries to practice in a more ethical manner, so its sales staff does not look bad by comparison, and bullies the good ones out of the business. There is just more money to be made by doing harm.

For those seeking an understanding of how so-called financial professionals can harm their clients, see "ABOUT YOUR FINAN-

CIAL MURDER…", a non fiction work by the author that began my quest to help protect the public. https://www.lulu.com/shop/larry-elford/about-your-financial-murder/paperback/product-23546465.html

Over 3000 financial employees came forward to CBC and told stories of being forced to do harm to the public, being forced to hide the role of salesperson, behind fancy, made up, but legally meaningless financial expert titles, being pressured to take advantage of customers vulnerability and trust.

I stand here in hopes that this government will take investor protection seriously, and use taxpayer resources to establish investor protection agencies in Canada. Agencies which are not 'captured by the industry' as most are today.

Today there are over 100 agencies, regulators, self regulators, or simple trade and lobby groups, who all say that they protect the public, most say this while not protecting the public at all. Most are mere marketing and PR slogans.

There are over 1500 employees at just the top four provincial securities commissions in Canada, and salaries to those 1500 people cost $230 million per year.

Why is it that four people at the CBC, and a couple of unpaid industry analysts must continue striving to protect Canada from financial predators?

When one considers the other 100 agencies who claim mandates of financial protection of Canadians, after watching the game for over 30 years now I feel qualified to offer an opinion:

Investment "regulatory" agencies who are funded by the investment industry, turn out to be more "insulators" or "buffers", to protect and distance the financial system from accountability, than protectors of the public.

I observe that every million dollars paid to regulators, returns up to a billion dollars in profit, back to financial institutions. Purchasing and owning the regulators may be the best investment anywhere...for financial predators. The cost to purchase all the regulatory bodies in the land is in the tenths-of-pennies for each dollar gained by owning the regulators.

I have also learned that financial systems do not repair themselves, instead they feed themselves. They profit handsomely by every flaw, and every intentional system design error. There is never a reason to change, since it works perfectly...for the players, just not for the country.

99% of what is touted as professional investment advice, or any other important sounding 'title', can be compared to the Ring Of Gyges, where the crimes of the holder of that ring are completely invisible, and the wearer can do anything desired, with no repercussions. Captured regulators exist to make that invisibility possible.

Most regulatory bodies in Canada that proclaim investor protection, simply serve as the Ring of Gyges, and on close inspection are often nothing more than a cloak to cover up systemic financial crime.

My local police chief suggested that the effects of organized crime is one of the biggest areas of crime growth that he is seeing at his street level....he said if I had one point to make in Ottawa, that criminals in suits are the ones behind the greatest harm to persons on his streets. He may have been thinking more about the drug traffickers than financial traffickers, but his City did lose 30 million from financial organized crime. No investigation, no charges.

A doctor I spoke with recently told me that it would make us weep, if we knew the patient epidemic of stress related issues that he is having to treat.
=========

When I did research for a documentary film about the unique violence of white collar crime, in 2005, I found over 100 financial bodies in Canada claiming to protect the public.

From my three or more decades of experience, I believe that in reality there is virtually no one in Canada charged with protecting the public from systemic financial abusers…the ones we trust with our money. I am sure there are one or two good agencies, the banking ombudsman used to come to mind, but they have since been forbidden to even touch systemic matters, so they have also been neutered by the system.

There is statistically zero effort to truly protect the public, since virtually all effort in Canada is done by agencies and regulatory bodies who are paid by financial industry money, and not by public money.

Larry Elford, Independent Investment Industry Analyst
End of 2017 Parliamentary Press Gallery Presentation
=========
Full presentation found on YouTube, titled "LARRY ELFORD PRESS conf OTTAWA June 7 2017 Ring of Gyges"

https://www.youtube.com/watch?v=-w8kjzLB4UE&t=9s

Video of the afternoon question and answer session within the Ottawa Parliamentary Finance Committee is found here for those who would like more on the story:

"Financial Systems Rigging, FINA Parliamentary testimony ELFORD June 7 2017"
https://www.youtube.com/watch?v=5kDQntFV5lw&t=37s

The investor is the brunette in the middle who thinks she is the customer, when in most cases, she is the "product" for the secret relationship between her "advisor" and the regulator that lets the industry mis-represent the "advisor" license and registration.

Chapter 2

The Evolution of Lawyers, 1500's

<u>This Chapter is about:</u> Expansion of the powers of the legal trade have evolved so slowly, as to be almost invisible to the public.

<u>It is important because:</u> The process of lawyer evolution, has occurred over Centuries, preventing people from ever realizing what has been taken from them over that time.

My friend Joe Killoran points out that corporations often use lawyers today as the hitmen and hushers of our time. In one case I witnessed, I watched a financial industry whistleblower (truthteller) driven to suicide by legal tactics that were both cruel and dishonest. Joe was involved in the case and refused to accept the lawless acts of the legal system. He was then sentenced to ten days in jail as punishment for standing up and questioning the court. He was called an "unwelcome interloper" by the lawyer who claimed to have made a million dollars in fees from the case. The legal dishonesty was successfully covered up using a blanket of money and the legal system. All guilty parties used the court to walk free.

The story of Jacob Fugger, The Richest Man In The World, is an interesting book for those wishing to better understand our systems. In it, Jacob Fugger's life and times are documented.
The book also touched upon the evolution of the legal profession and the expanding role of lawyers in the 1500's.

This chapter contains excerpts from The Richest Man In The World, written by Greg Steinmetz. These book-excerpts are shown in text boxes like the one below.

> *"Capitalism was moving faster than society's ability to contain it."*
> *"While commerce was barreling ahead, democratic institutions that could have curbed the excesses revolved more slowly, allowing well-connected men like Fugger to have their way regardless of other considerations"*
>
> *"Into that time stepped Jacob Fugger, called the first modern plutocrat, as well as the first modern capitalist, the man who wrote the playbook for everyone who keeps score using money."*

Was his playbook written fairly or unfairly? When is it time for a rewrite, or do we simply let clever men create rigged belief systems, and then let those rigged systems benefit clever men forever? What about the harm to society?

Fugger's business practices, along with the reactions of a man named Martin Luther, caused some of the greatest changes in history. It was Jacob Fugger's money which indebted the Catholic Church enough for them to begin selling indulgences to repay the loans.

> *"The Reformation had many causes, Vatican corruption, lustful priests and church meddling in secular affairs all fed the rebelling against the Catholic church. But Fugger lit the fuse."*
> *"His man had an idea. They suggested a church financing device called an indulgence..."*

Jacob Fugger might be considered the original "Payday Lender", who pushed the church into enough debt to require the sale of indulgences to pay that debt back.

For those not aware, "indulgences" were the "get out of hell" passes that the Catholic Church began selling to raise money, and which triggered Martin Luther to protest, triggering the great upheaval called the Reformation. The timeline was 15th Century.

An 'indulgence' was part of the medieval Christian church, and a significant trigger to the Protestant Reformation. Basically, by purchasing an indulgence, an individual could reduce the length and severity of punishment that heaven would require as payment for their sins, or so the church claimed.

By challenging the authority of the Pope in 1517, Martin Luther brought about the end of Christian unity in Western Europe. The resulting Protestant Reformation changed the course of Western civilization.

The Reformation is considered to have started with the publication of the *Ninety-five Theses* by Martin Luther in 1517, where he directly opposed and challenged the Roman Catholic church for its practices. The printing press had recently been invented which allowed, for the first time, ordinary persons to spread printed words far and wide. This ability was a bit of an equalizer between the powers that be, and the new power of public awareness.

The evolution of lawyers is also discussed in the story of The Richest Man In The World:

"The Renaissance gave rise to a new breed of professionals that instantly won the scorn of the general public. The people hated their haughty manners and fancy robes. They hated their use of Latin and their bewildering arguments. Hutton called them "empty wind bags". Another writer likened them to locusts: "They are increasing like grasshoppers year by year."

"Another remarked on their ability to sow chaos: 'In my home there is but one and yet his wiles bring the whole country around here into confusion. What a misery this hoard brings upon us.'"

Who were these wind bags, locusts and misery bringers? They were, of course, lawyers. Arising from the swamps of canon law, they made their secular debut in Fugger's lifetime. They arose because the emergence of capitalism and the growth of trade necessitated a new, modern body of law and practitioners to make sense of it."

"The old legal system, known as customary law, used common sense to settle disputes and torture to extract confessions. It worked well enough on feudal estates where everyone knew each other, but failed to keep pace as a society transition from the medieval to the modern. Rather than develop a new system, society adapted an existing system that was robust enough for commerce and dovetailed with the Renaissance love of everything ancient. This was Roman law as set of laws Emperor Justinian I, fortified in 529 to govern the empire and apply common rules from Egypt to England."

Roman and customary law took contrary views of property rights. Customary law, based on Christian values, saw property as communal. To the extent anyone owned anything, it came with the duty to share. The peasants who plowed the Lord's fields could hunt in those fields and fish in his streams."

"Everything belonged to everyone. Roman law, on the other hand, honored the individual over the communal and emphasized the privileges of property ownership instead of the duties."

"The Roman system went hand in hand with capitalism because it included private ownership of property. The princes liked the Roman system because it put property in their hands and left them with more than they had before."

"The rich merchants liked it because they discovered that a good lawyer could use clever arguments to defeat common sense and win cases they should have lost."

I began writing this book after finishing up a book project titled, "ABOUT YOUR FINANCIAL MURDER...". I had come to realize that the financial and investment industry were allowed to ransack the public by as much wealth as all other criminal acts. From personal experience inside the investment industry, I saw that retail investors (moms and pops) were being "farmed" of generous portions of their money, rather than being given the promised financial "advice", or even a licensed adviser.

Being an inside witness to this sensitized me to how corporations do this and get away with it. A common element required in pillage of the public is lawyers. Whether industry lawyers, or regulatory lawyers, the effect was the same. The industry was allowed to win every time, while being insulated from accountability when harming customers.

Financial industry lawyers rigged the game, and regulatory industry lawyers (SEC, OSC, ASC, and hundreds of others) are paid to play along. Any regulatory employee knows that if they "play along" and do the bidding of the industry, their chances for promotion to industry jobs is enhanced. The corruption of systemic organized crime is thus self-reinforcing.

For me it felt like I imagine any ethical Boeing employee felt in the years prior to 2020, as the safety of the product (737 Max) is thrown overboard by executives to enrich themselves. Billions were funnelled to executives and shareholders, while one of America's great companies was strip-farmed.
The deeper I looked at ransacking the public, the more it resembled professionally-organized crimes.

Lawyers created the concept of "invisible friends", otherwise known as corporations, who could not be arrested or jailed, since they did not exist, except on paper. In a game of "lets pretend...", that lawyers seem good at, anything that can be imagined, can be tested on the public...just like an unsafe aircraft.

Corporations are a construct of three things. Firstly a construct of the human mind. Secondly, they become real when a lawyer puts this construct down on paper, and pushes it through the system. The third "construct" is when society accepts or agrees to go along, unwittingly or otherwise. The public is trained to obey or accept what the courts decide, since they still hold a level of trust in the legal system. Are we falling for the trick of believing men in robes again, and are they selling us self-serving belief systems... again?

Corporations could be imagined as if they were a derivative, something artificial created, and which is "derived" from something real or imagined. *"Hey, lets pretend that corporations have all the rights of persons, but you cannot handcuff or arrest them. What could go wrong?"*

If we go back to the origins of corporations, we find endless maneuvers that have succeeded in bringing fees to lawyers, endless gain to corporations, and disadvantage for most of humanity, except for the 1% who own corporations.

How are mere mortals expected to compete, survive and thrive, in a world where lawyers have created a superior-status, paper-created artifice, with ability to avoid arrest and accountability for its actions? A Ring of Gyges created by lawyers.

For those who mistake my words for condemnation of corporations, please understand that it is not the corporation I oppose, but rather aspects of the legal protection built into corporations, which allow them to walk, talk and work freely among the public, as if they were a human entity, but allow its owners to walk away richer...by harming the public. The owners of the corporation can simply say, "I did not do it, my invisible friend did..."

(Credit to Legal Scholar and Professor Harry Glasbeek for the "invisible friend" quote)

Chapter 3

Capitalism Verses Lawless Capitalism

<u>This Chapter is about:</u> The difference between Capitalism governed by the rule of law, and Lawless Capitalism governed by corrupt systems or tricks.

<u>It is important because:</u> If the system is broken, perhaps it is not capitalism at fault, but perhaps it has been over-run by corrupt system actors. We should try to understand what is broken before judgement.

If Capitalism could be summed up in a simple principle it might be: **Capitalism provides the greatest rewards to those who do the greatest good for the greatest number of people.** *It is also very much about freedom of choice and free markets.*

The invisible hand guides people to do what would best serve their own economic interests, and in a lawful society, the thing that would best serve any man's interest is to make a lot of money by doing the most good, for the most people. The principles are almost too simple to screw up, and they follow economist Adam Smith's analogy of the "invisible hand of the markets".

Today, thanks to man-made belief systems, some men can elevate themselves and hide behind artificial persons. It allows men to earn greater rewards by doing harm to humans and to our planet. After all, who can stop them, if they have an "invisible friend" doing the harm?

This is "Lawless Capitalism" and it should not be mistaken for "Capitalism" in any way. It is the lawlessness that allows the farming of humans, and not Capitalism itself.

Jacob Fugger, "having his way" with the public and governments, triggering wars, and holding the Catholic Church hostage to debt, led me to imagine the concept of how easily it is to corral humans into man-made belief systems.

Today, we have capitalism, without enforcement of laws for persons at the top. We have lawless capitalism for a select few, which is as bad as any corrupt or criminal system imaginable. It is as criminal as lawless socialism would be, or corrupt communism. Each simply creates artificial powers capable of abusing society.

Lawlessness causes systemic unfairness in society, and with all things unfair, society is permitted to ask the question, "If it is designed to be unfair, then is it even legitimate? Does it deserve obedience?"

I should back up one notch and make a distinction between lawyers who serve people and lawyers who serve corporations. I am not sure what to say, other than my feelings of animosity does not often apply to professionals who serve people, lawyers included, but when service to corporations becomes involved, an enhanced level of rapaciousness seems reached. Corporate lawyers seem to rise to a higher level of predation, even when it involves harming people. Are corporate lawyers some kind of derivative of the legal profession? *(see"What does it mean if something is a derivative?" on page 271)*

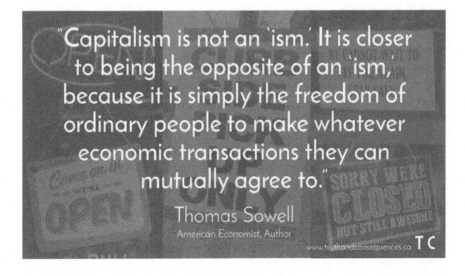

"Capitalism is not an 'ism.' It is closer to being the opposite of an 'ism,' because it is simply the freedom of ordinary people to make whatever economic transactions they can mutually agree to."

Thomas Sowell
American Economist, Author

www.truthandconsequences.ca   T C

COULD A PROFANITY HAVE BEGUN WITH A BANKER?

The name "Fugger", may have brought about one of the world's strongest profanities used to express emotion. I throw it out there not to prove a point, but to explore the possibility, since some of this book is about thought experiments of "lets pretend…"

Based upon ruthless tactics by which Jacob Fugger became the richest man in the world, it is not hard to picture him being well hated by many. ("Don't be such a Fugger")

Greg Steinmetz's book contains more than one quote to suggest that the word "Fugger" could have began a common statement of disgust. Searches for the origins of the "F" word, suggest Germanic origins from the time period that fits this story (1500's).

In an open letter to the German nobility (1520), Martin Luther pleads with the princes to crack down on big business. This time, Luther dispenses with the generalities and attacks Fugger directly: "We must put a bit in the mouth of the Fugger."

In another quote in the book after Archduke Ferdinand found a financial backer, he wrote of the news saying, *"we inform you that we have arranged to borrow from the Fuggers."*

Perhaps today's economic system of "lawless capitalism" is a bit like the 1500's, when in Greg Steinmetz's words:

"Capitalism was moving faster than society's ability to contain it."

"While commerce was barreling ahead, democratic institutions that could have curbed the excesses revolved more slowly, allowing well-connected men like Fugger to have their way regardless of other considerations"

Chapter 4

Why Are Lawyers Always Involved...in Harming Humans?

This Chapter is about: The strange coincidence of often seeing lawyers involved in serious systemic crime. Trick #2 for Farming Humans is to have so-called professionals create rigged or self serving systems of belief.

It is important because: What if what we call "professionals" are just men in robes, acting out a role?

In the book **"No One Would Listen"**, by Harry Markopolos, the author tried to interest SEC lawyers in the Bernie Madoff scam, for about a decade. Nothing happened. His book is worth reading to see inside sycophantic power systems like the SEC (U.S. Securities Exchange Commission). His observations about lawyers say a great deal about some of the public-harms that lawyers are sometimes employed to do.

Some select quotes from his book in italics below:

> *"First, banish the lawyers from the land."*
> *"Lawyers need to be removed from most positions of senior leadership..."*
> *"The typical SEC attorney would have trouble finding fireworks on the 4 of July..."*

His book should be seen today as a warning of what corporate milkmaids and handmaids are draining from societies every day.

(Milkmaid is term used to describe persons who "milk systems better", while pretending to "make systems better")

Lawyers who serve corporate interests are often incentivized to create complex, financial and legal constructs, which act as

siphons to drain society of freedom, money, hopes and dreams.

They disguise these traps so the are not seen as traps, but as clever advantages for corporate clients. If nothing gets physically taken away from the man on the street, while corporations gain powers unavailable to the average person, lawyers can create social inequality out of thin air, like bankers can literally create money out of thin air using fractional reserve lending.

What if the addition of such belief systems, or systems of "make believe" elevates persons who own corporations above our system of laws? Or, to be more precise, what if laws that apply to mortals, are not applied to persons who direct corporations to commit illegal acts, including acts which cause war, death, disease etc.

Doesn't that give them superior powers above ordinary persons, almost like the Ring of Gyges? Isn't that equivalent to putting a yoke, a chain or invisible weights upon the backs of those have no access to those make-believe powers?

That is how to farm humans, using artificial belief systems created out of thin air. Systems which serve only some humans and not others. Again, we must ask if systems of justice and governance are being skewed to serve only some men and not others, are they even legitimate? Have we selectively repealed "all men are created equal", the most important principle in the Declaration of Independence.

Corporations are considered to be "persons" in some respects, but without the burden of accountability and responsibility of every other member of humanity.

I wonder if it appears to some as a trap? But a trap designed in such a way that only humans can fall into. From my experience with professional corporate crime, and the systemic impunity of most or all of those crimes, billions of people in the world today are caught in such a trap. An invisible trap created for select people only. What could go wrong? Everything can and will go wrong until principles of human fairness are restored.

More recently (2017) on the timeline comes this quote from a former Royal Canadian Mounted Police (RCMP) money laundering expert:

"......the Canadian Bar Association is probably the most powerful criminal organization in Canada..."
Former RCMP Inspector Bill Majcher,

See Youtube Video titled: *"France is Lost, The Fix is In: Gerald Celente & RCMP Inspector Bill Majcher" (1:20:00 on video)*

Did lawyers create the first "derivatives"?
Are corporate lawyers themselves derivatives?
Of what? *(see" What does it mean if something is a derivative?"
on page 271)*

Could lawyers in robes, speaking at times in Latin, like priests of old, inventing laws and rules, to create real-world favors for their clients, be simple character actors, playing a role which we have all been convinced to believe? A game of pretend?

What if some creations of these robed men and women, are nothing more than "belief systems" which society must then adhere to? What if some belief systems are nothing more than rigged rules and legislated unfairness? What if you could invent, enact or alter laws to more effectively farm humans? You could easily become a billionaire...and a serial society-killer.

Don't worry if that concept makes you shake your head, I am only trying to better understand it myself. But the thought of artificially created, "intangible things", actors if you will, given such influence in society, seems a bit like some of the derivative financial products that society has begun to wise up to, and to question as well.

Professor Harry J. Glasbeek, is Professor Emeritus of Osgoode Hall Law School of York University in Toronto. His work covers a lifetime of study and teaching the law. I first met him in 2004 when he was on a speaking tour for his then new book, "Wealth By Stealth", Corporate Crime, Corporate Law, and the Perversion of Democracy.

His presentation resonated then and has become ever more relevant as time goes on. When I heard him speak, he made quite an impression about how belief systems and legal systems create entities which are above our laws. It allows owners of corporations who do great harm to continue pocketing the money, but avoid prosecution with a defense that sounds a lot like "I did not do it, my invisible friend did".

The CEO of Boeing gained $60 million dollars for himself, by cutting costs, corners and safety, on the new 727 MAX in 2020. The harm was when two newly designed aircraft and hundreds of passengers flew into the ground, as a result. The ability to say "I did not do it, my invisible friend did", allows the attributes of the Ring of Gyges to flow millions of dollars to owners and executives, without accountability for the harm to the public. After all, they did not do it,…their invisible friend did.

Some will ask me how this applies to the topic of the book, which is "Farming Humans", and to that I say the following: If owners and executives in a billion dollar corporation can evade personal accountability for causing injury or death, while earning millions by taking shortcuts and actions to benefit the corporation, then lawyers have created a creature which can do harm, but not "do time". A modern day "Ring of Gyges."

By way of a second answer, lets look at how executive compensation packages (also designed by lawyers and lobby groups) led to the pillage of economies and societies.

"Lets first remove any laws that say that corporations or executives of corporations cannot manipulate their share price on the stock market, using corporate money…and in step two, we will write executive compensation contracts based partially on how well the stock price does…by granting executives options to purchase company shares to give them incentives to improve the value of the company. That sounds reasonable right?" Companies went ahead and granted key executives options to purchase a certain number of corporate shares at a fixed price, to incentivize their executives and give them more "skin in the game".

The only trouble with this is executives soon figured out the trick to gaming the system and gaining millions of dollars. If they held one million options to buy their company shares for $100, when the shares were trading at $90, this perk was worthless to them. What to do?

One thing was to toss assets overboard, sell key assets, borrow to raise even more money and begin buying their own shares on the stock market. Executives went into the stock market-manipulation game for their own shares while they quietly stripped and pawned their own companies. Some of America's best companies were hollowed out, just so the executives could push the share price higher and higher. Increased dividend payouts also had the effect of stripping cash from the company while raising the stock market price.

In the end, with the share price now up to $150 from all the stripping, buying shares on the markets, decreasing the number of shares outstanding, increasing dividends, etc., the executive's one million share options are now worth $50 million dollars.

This is Trick #3 in Farming Humans. Making it legal for insider manipulation of public markets for private insider gain.

Harry Glasbeek is Professor Emeritus and Senior Scholar at Osgoode Hall Law School, York University. He has also taught at the Universities of Melbourne and Monash in Australia, and the University of Western Ontario. He is the author of ten books including Wealth by Stealth: Corporate Crime, Corporate Law, and the Perversion of Democracy.

Chapter 5

Justice Follows Laws of Gravity?

This Chapter is about: Man-made belief systems (laws) today allow some persons to be "more equal than others". Many of these "more equal" persons are able to fly above the law.

It is important because: Justice and power finds it safer to prosecute in a downward direction, which often leaves none policing those above. This can give a free pass to systemic criminality done by those in power and influence. (Trick #4 in Farming Humans: Justice prefers to look only down…rarely up towards power)

Imagine this fictional thought experiment if you can: Picture yourself as a young person who has just obtained your dream job. You are hired to become a firefighter and the training process has begun. You are as happy as you have ever been and full of hope for your new career.

Everything flows along for a few years, and you are immersed in learning the ropes and fitting in with the crews. Then something strange happens. You begin to see signs that a few people above you, people that you count upon as your superiors, are doing the occasional moonlighting job of arson for hire. What a mind blowing discovery for a young person, to learn that the people you trust the most, are running a side business of starting fires, behind their public role of fighting fires. But who better to hire as an arsonist as firemen and arson inspectors? Of course this does not happen in the real world, so before you quit this story in disgust, please keep in mind that this is only a thought experiment.

You also learn that your superiors are testing you, to find out if you can be trusted to "be a team player", trusted to not reveal their activities. What do you do? Do you do the right thing, and reveal the crimes, or do you remain silent and keep your job?
I cannot tell you that something like this has ever occurred, I know that similar has taken place in the ranks of many police agencies,

and in the corporate world this kind of dilemma happens every day. Entire libraries could be filled with stories of Wall Street, Bay Street or any other financial district where cheating the public has become more profitable than providing honest services to the public. CEO's have become famous for stripping their own companies from within, even at the cost of human lives. I witnessed this type of double-bind every day in my career in the retail investment industry, and I can assure readers that it continues today, due to the magic of "self" regulation.

What does this story have to do with a natural law like gravity?

Applying justice is like shining a light on a situation, so that all can see what is happening. Illuminating the problem is the first step in fixing the problem. But the most difficult and dangerous thing at times, is to shine a light upon ones peers, or even more dangerous, to shine a light upwards on ones superiors. The man at the bottom knows that those at the top have invisible connections and methods by which to not only escape justice, but to punish those who dare to be disloyal.

For these reasons, justice and power usually follow the law of gravity, always making the light of justice fall down upon those below. Never upward to the top, and never sideways on ones own peers. Those could be a real career killer.

In addition to the risks of applying justice and law to those in power and wealth, the creation of artificial persons (corporations) with powers of limited liability etc., have caused a repeal of the natural principles of poverty and prosperity. Prosperity has been tilted more easily towards those who did not earn it, and poverty toward those who did nothing to deserve it. Getting away with financial murder on society is simple, when we combine the powers of a corporation, with the gravitational pull that causes accountability to apply downward, and rarely upward to the source of the greatest crimes upon society. That is why farming humans is so easy on a grand scale. No one can touch the systemic crime players that rig the entire system.

Another way to express how that works is seen in the old saying, "big dogs don't bite big dogs". You can see this in action as police and prosecutors also follow the principles of gravity, usually applying their power downward upon those least likely to cause a backlash. Almost never is a president or a prime minister, or billionaire CEO pursued with as much vigor as a street criminal, despite a single CEO easily able to do the economic harm of *fifty thousand street crimes in one blow. There is just too much risk of career backlash when wealthy, powerful or influential persons are pursued.

This may be why a public accountability movement, mentioned in the solutions area of this book, could offer hope. It might allow a workaround for the problem that justice has in dealing with top dollar crimes. More on that later.

The $60 Million dollar "parting gift" to Boeing's CEO in 2019, is roughly equivalent to the economic cost of twelve thousand average street crimes. And yet we spend mere tenths of pennies on policing the rich and powerful above us, when compared to what society spends to put their knee on the necks of those below.

Try to imagine the number of street crimes it would take to equal the cost to society of the Trillions siphoned to private banks by the Federal Reserve…which is privately owned by those same banks. I get an equivalent of one Billion average street crimes in 2020 alone, but don't take my word for it.

* Fifty thousand street crimes (or property crime) at an average cost of $5000 each, amounts to two hundred and fifty million dollars. A white collar criminal can easily do crime in tens of billions. "The Cost of Crime to Society: New Crime-Specific Estimates for Policy and Program Evaluation")
Kathryn E. McCollister,a Michael T. French,b and Hai Fangc

Chapter 6   1775

The American Revolutionary War

This Chapter is about: The U.S. fought to become a country be-cause it's people grew tired of being "Farmed" by Britain.

It is important because: America (and other countries) is being farmed once again, this time by laws and belief systems created by clever men who claim to serve the public .

The American Revolutionary War was fought between Great Britain and the original Thirteen British colonies in North America. People in the Thirteen Colonies disliked many actions of the British Government, such as the Intolerable Acts. The British gov-ernment chose which countries the colonies could trade with, in-stead of the colonies deciding it themselves. Colonists wanted freedom to make their own trade decisions. (Note to self: Never tell Bostonians where they can or cannot obtain their tea.)

In 1765, the British Parliament needed money to pay back the debt for the French and Indian War. They passed a Law called the Stamp Act. This law said that colonists had to buy stamps for legal papers, newspapers, and even playing cards, as other British people did. The money from the stamps went to the King. The colonies did not follow this law. The colonies kept refusing to do what the King wanted. The Boston Tea Party and Boston Mas-sacre caused people to become more angry about the situation. The British sent more soldiers (Red Coats) to keep control of the colonies and they sometimes had to fight. In 1774, the British passed the Intolerable Acts.

The Intolerable Acts consisted of a number of measures meant to punish the port of Boston and the people of Massachusetts for the Boston Tea party. Parliament, now under the leadership of Lord North, passed the first of these measures, the Boston Port Act, in March 1774. This act provided that the port of Boston would be closed until the East India Company received compensation for the loss of the tea and the Royal Government received payment for the lost income it would have received on the customs duty.

The second of these laws was known as the Administration of Justice Act of 1774. This act allowed a change of venue to another British colony or to Great Britain for trials of officials charged with a crime growing out of their enforcement of the law or suppression of riots. The third of the Intolerable Acts, the Massachusetts Government Act, abolished the popularly elected upper council of the colony and replaced them with a 12 to 36 member council appointed by the King of England.
https://www.historyisfun.org/learn/learning-center/what-were-the-intolerable-acts/

The American Revolution came to an end in 1783 when a peace treaty was signed in Paris, France. In the Treaty of Paris, the British King, George III accepted the independence of the colonies and recognized the newly created nation as the United States of America.

The treaty also gave all the land Britain said it owned which was west of the Appalachians as far as the Mississippi River to the new country. This land would eventually become part of the US, and lead to the creation of 35 new states (some of which later rebelled as part of the Confederate States of America) that now make up the contiguous United States. Many British Loyalists fled to Canada.

The United States of America became a country because the people had become tired of being financially "farmed" by Britain. 150 years later they are again being farmed…only the farmers today are their most trusted leaders, professionals and institutions.

CHAPTER 7   1832
The US Civil War

This Chapter is about: 180 years ago or more, banks were ag-
gressively pursuing efforts to enslave Americans into debt and to
farm them of interest forever. Think "Payday Lending", 1800's
style. This is Trick #5 in the game of Farming Humans.

It is important because: Presidents have been killed so that
bankers could capture perhaps the greatest powers on earth.
Power #1 is sole-franchise-permition to create every US dollar
ever created...and be paid for creating them. Power #2 is the ability to collect interest on the debt used to "back" those dollars.
Power #3 is the ability to lend ten times the amount of those dollars which were then deposited into their own banks, under "fractional reserve lending". The bankers seem to have won the ability
to farm humans on nearly every count.

> "...by 1860, there were more millionaires (slaveholders all) living in
> the lower Mississippi Valley than anywhere else in the United
> States. In the same year, the nearly 4 million American slaves
> were worth some $3.5 billion, making them the largest single fi-
> nancial asset in the entire U.S. economy, worth more than all
> manufacturing and railroads combined."
>
> From recordings of David Blight's course at Yale, The Civil War
> and Reconstruction   http://www.davidwblight.com/teaching

Physical slavery was an early example of Farming Humans. Today
we have done away with physical slavery, but we accepted new
belief systems that create forms of slavery without chains. Economic slavery is one example.

In this chapter I began to understand why all wars could truly be
bankers wars, as is said in a video by Zane Henry based on a radio show by Michael Rivero. (Search "ALL WARS ARE
BANKERS' WARS" on Youtube for this man's unique perspective)

A common explanation is that the Civil War was fought over the moral issue of slavery. In reality, much of it was the economics of slavery and political control of that system that was central to the conflict.

Slaves were a substantial source of wealth through the labour they provided to slave owners. They were the fuel that propelled the farming industry that used slaves. Imagine a president today threatening to ban the diesel fuel needed by farmers today. It would trigger a fight.

With cash crops of tobacco, cotton and sugar cane, America's southern states became the economic engine of the burgeoning nation. Their fuel of choice? Human slavery.
GREG TIMMONS

Andrew Jackson became President of the United States in 1832. He spoke out against the establishment of a national bank, after the election, taking a stand against grants of monopolies and exclusive privileges, against "prostitution of our government" to the advancement of the few at the expense of the many. He recognized the financiers motivations to financially enslave America in debt to bankers, and he prevented it from happening...for a while.

In 1835, President Jackson paid off the final installment on the US national debt. His accomplishment was something that had never been done before, and has never been done since. America was a debt free nation. Jackson had beaten the banks who had sought to enslave America with debt.

This was followed by attempts to assassinate Jackson, which failed.

Next comes Lincoln who carried on with the desire to not enrich private bankers by trapping the States into their debt schemes. He instead printed government issued "United States Notes", called greenbacks due to the color of the ink used in the printing.

The Greenbacks were government receipts given for work done or goods delivered, so the greenbacks represented man hours of work already done, and they could be traded in the community for other goods and services. Thus a simple government-backed currency was born into being without any need for bankers.

To then fund the Civil War between States, banks were offering the government millions of dollars at interest costs of 24 to 36 percent. Lincoln knew that such loans would be impossible to repay, and he chose instead to let the government print its own money rather than borrow from bankers. This thinking met the "true genius is found in simplicity" test. https://addicted2success.com/quotes/41-essential-quotes-that-shows-the-beauty-of-simplicity/

Lincoln also feared the financial slavery that bankers wished to trap the country in, for their own gain.

In 1972, the US Treasury Department was asked to compute the cost to government if the money had been borrowed from banks instead of being simply printed by the government. They calculated that Lincoln had saved the US a total of $4 billion in interest, just by printing $400 million in Greenbacks rather than borrowing that money from bankers.

Government issued Greenbacks were simple, debt-free legal government tender that did not have to be paid back to bankers.

Thomas Edison said to the New York times in 1921, "If a nation can issue a dollar bond, it can issue a dollar bill. The same element that makes the bond good, makes the bill good also. It is absurd to say our country can issue bonds and cannot issue currency. Both are promises to pay, but one fattens the usurer and the other helps the people."

Meanwhile, the bankers of the time were driven and determined to split the federation apart so that they could finance two separate sides of the civil war, and earn a fortune in interest for themselves.

Banks throughout history have sought control of as much government debt as possible, knowing that starting wars is one of the easiest methods of putting a government into debt.

Debt kept governments under control of the banks, and earned the banks a share of all the labour of the nation in the form of interest payments. It is like having a free income for life, for a bank, when they bury a country in debt and collect interest forever.

"Slavery is but the owning of labour..," page 62 of the book "Web of Debt".

Lincoln fought to prevent private bankers from putting the nation into this type of debt.

Lincoln was assassinated in 1865.

Banks throughout history seem willing to kill to gain their financial advantage. Don't take my word for it, Search "All Wars Are Bankers Wars" on YouTube and make your own conclusions.

Portions of this chapter were sourced from the book "Web of Debt", by Ellen H. Brown, J.D.

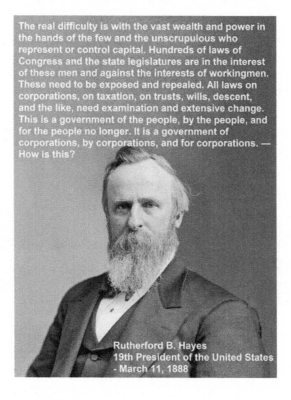

The real difficulty is with the vast wealth and power in the hands of the few and the unscrupulous who represent or control capital. Hundreds of laws of Congress and the state legislatures are in the interest of these men and against the interests of workingmen. These need to be exposed and repealed. All laws on corporations, on taxation, on trusts, wills, descent, and the like, need examination and extensive change. This is a government of the people, by the people, and for the people no longer. It is a government of corporations, by corporations, and for corporations. — How is this?

Rutherford B. Hayes
19th President of the United States
- March 11, 1888

Chapter 8   1886
Corporations Are Now "Persons"

<u>This Chapter is about:</u>   Corporate lawyers invent a new "belief system" which creates a entirely new class of "person". This is Trick # 6 in the game of Farming Humans, to create something which gives a few men an elevated status above the rest.

<u>It is important because:</u> It created a "superior-being" and the diminishing side-effects upon "human persons" is felt to this day.

1776 "All men are created equal". Declaration of Independence. 1886 The creation of artificial persons, who could not be arrested, handcuffed, or jailed. What could go wrong?

Wouldn't that be a win for any law firm, to create a modern day Ring of Gyges for it's clients? To create a special cloak which gave them elevated powers beyond all humans, protection from arrest. How do you arrest a company? I wonder what the unintended side effects could be for society, 130 years later?

Let's look back at the creation of artificial people. To do this we visit the 1800s, when the Southern Pacific Railroad company was owned by a robber baron named Leland Stanford.

> "Robber baron" is a derogatory metaphor of social criticism origi-
> nally applied to certain late 19th-century American businessmen
> who were accused of using unscrupulous methods to get rich, or
> expand their wealth. Wikipedia

After California lawmakers placed a special tax on Southern Pacific's land, the railroad company protested, arguing that this tax was
an act of discrimination under the 14th amendment.

The amendment guarantees every "Person" the equal protection
of the law. In a bizarre twist of logic that appears to be a source of
some of the increasing poverty in modern (2020) society, this
company, and it's lawyers, set in motion the creation of artificial
persons. Anyone reading this today might see the lunacy of such
logic, however corporate lawyers were simply coming up with
unique ways to add to their firm's billings…as they continue doing
to this day.

The argument made by lawyers for the Southern Pacific Railroad
was that the railroad corporation was a "person", and because the
Constitution protected all persons from discrimination, it must also
protect the southern Pacific Railway from discrimination on its
property tax bill.

It seems that lawyers slipped in the "Corporations are persons"
issue, in a thought experiment to solve a tax issue. Another game
of lawyers playing, "Lets pretend….", and the unintended side effects were creation of artificial, unstoppable giants, who now dominate the majority of power and wealth on the planet.

This might be something that we might want to "revisit", if our society is to survive the next 100 years.

The following are excerpts from The Atlantic by Adam Winkler:

'Corporations Are People' Is Built on an Incredible 19th-Century Lie

How a farcical series of events in the 1880s produced an enduring and controversial legal precedent
ADAM WINKLER

MAR 5, 2018 The Atlantic

A 1907 caricature of the railroad baron Edward H. Harriman swallowing America's train lines. LUTHER BRADLEY / LIBRARY OF CONGRESS / CORBIS / GETTY

Somewhat unintuitively, American corporations today enjoy many of the same rights as American citizens. Both, for instance, are entitled to the freedom of speech and the freedom of religion. How exactly did corporations come to be understood as "people" bestowed with the most fundamental constitutional rights? The answer can be found in a bizarre—even farcical—series of lawsuits over 130 years ago involving a lawyer who lied to the Supreme

Court, an ethically challenged justice, and one of the most powerful corporations of the day.

That corporation was the Southern Pacific Railroad Company, owned by the robber baron Leland Stanford. In 1881, after California lawmakers imposed a special tax on railroad property, Southern Pacific pushed back, making the bold argument that the law was an act of unconstitutional discrimination under the Fourteenth Amendment. Adopted after the Civil War to protect the rights of the freed slaves, that amendment guarantees to every "person" the "equal protection of the laws." Stanford's railroad argued that it was a person too, reasoning that just as the Constitution prohibited discrimination on the basis of racial identity, so did it bar discrimination against Southern Pacific on the basis of its corporate identity.

The head lawyer representing Southern Pacific was a man named Roscoe Conkling. A leader of the Republican Party for more than a decade, Conkling had even been nominated to the Supreme Court twice. He begged off both times, the second time after the Senate had confirmed him. (He remains the last person to turn down a Supreme Court seat after winning confirmation). More than most lawyers, Conkling was seen by the justices as a peer.

It was a trust Conkling would betray. As he spoke before the Court on Southern Pacific's behalf, Conkling recounted an astonishing tale. In the 1860s, when he was a young congressman, Conkling had served on the drafting committee that was responsible for writing the Fourteenth Amendment. Then the last member of the committee still living, Conkling told the justices that the drafters had changed the wording of the amendment, replacing "citizens" with "persons" in order to cover corporations too. Laws referring to "persons," he said, have "by long and constant acceptance … been held to embrace artificial persons as well as natural persons." Conkling buttressed his account with a surprising piece of evidence: a musty old journal he claimed was a previously unpublished record of the deliberations of the drafting committee.

Years later, historians would discover that Conkling's journal was real but his story was a fraud. The journal was in fact a record of the congressional committee's deliberations but, upon close examination, it offered no evidence that the drafters intended to protect corporations. It showed, in fact, that the language of the equal-protection clause was never changed from "citizen" to "person." So far as anyone can tell, the rights of corporations were not raised in the public debates over the ratification of the Fourteenth Amendment or in any of the states' ratifying conventions. And, prior to Conkling's appearance on behalf of Southern Pacific, no member of the drafting committee had ever suggested that corporations were covered.

There's reason to suspect Conkling's deception was uncovered back in his time too. The justices held onto the case for three years without ever issuing a decision, until Southern Pacific unexpectedly settled the case. Then, shortly after, another case from Southern Pacific reached the Supreme Court, raising the exact same legal question. The company had the same team of lawyers, with the exception of Conkling. Tellingly, Southern Pacific's lawyers omitted any mention of Conkling's drafting history or his journal. Had those lawyers believed Conkling, it would have been malpractice to leave out his story.

When the Court issued its decision on this second case, the justices expressly declined to decide if corporations were people. The dispute could be, and was, resolved on other grounds, prompting an angry rebuke from one justice, Stephen J. Field, who castigated his colleagues for failing to address "the important constitutional questions involved." "At the present day, nearly all great enterprises are conducted by corporations," he wrote, and they deserved to know if they had equal rights too.

Rumored to carry a gun with him at all times, the colorful Field was the only sitting justice ever arrested—and the charge was murder. He was innocent, but nonetheless guilty of serious ethical violations in the Southern Pacific cases, at least by modern standards: A confidant of Leland Stanford, Field had advised the company on which lawyers to hire for this very series of cases and thus should have recused himself from them. He refused to—and, even worse, while the first case was pending, covertly shared internal memoranda of the justices with Southern Pacific's legal team.

The rules of judicial ethics were not well developed in the Gilded Age, however, and the self-assured Field, who feared the forces of socialism, did not hesitate to weigh in. Taxing the property of railroads differently, he said, was like allowing deductions for property "owned by white men or by old men, and not deducted if owned by black men or young men."

So, with Field on the Court, still more twists were yet to come. The Supreme Court's opinions are officially published in volumes edited by an administrator called the reporter of decisions. By tradition, the reporter writes up a summary of the Court's opinion and includes it at the beginning of the opinion. The reporter in the 1880s was J.C. Bancroft Davis, whose wildly inaccurate summary of the Southern Pacific case said that the Court had ruled that "corporations are persons within ... the Fourteenth Amendment." Whether his summary was an error or something more nefarious—Davis had once been the president of the Newburgh and New York Railway Company—will likely never be known.

Field nonetheless saw Davis's erroneous summary as an opportunity. A few years later, in an opinion in an unrelated case, Field wrote that "corporations are persons within the meaning" of the Fourteenth Amendment. "It was so held in Santa Clara County v. Southern Pacific Railroad," explained Field, who knew very well that the Court had done no such thing.

His gambit worked. In the following years, the case would be cited over and over by courts across the nation, including the Supreme Court, for deciding that corporations had rights under the Fourteenth Amendment.

Indeed, the faux precedent in the Southern Pacific case would go on to be used by a Supreme Court that in the early 20th century became famous for striking down numerous economic regulations, including federal child-labor laws, zoning laws, and wage-and-hour laws. Meanwhile, in cases like the notorious Plessy v. Ferguson (1896), those same justices refused to read the Constitution as protecting the rights of African Americans, the real intended beneficiaries of the Fourteenth Amendment. Between 1868, when the amendment was ratified, and 1912, the Supreme Court would rule on 28 cases involving the rights of African Americans and an astonishing 312 cases on the rights of corporations.

The day back in 1882 when the Supreme Court first heard Roscoe Conkling's argument, the New-York Daily Tribune featured a story on the case with a headline that would turn out to be prophetic: "Civil Rights of Corporations." Indeed, in a feat of deceitful legal alchemy, Southern Pacific and its wily legal team had, with the help of an audacious Supreme Court justice, set up the Four-teenth Amendment to be more of a bulwark for the rights of busi-nesses than the rights of minorities.

ADAM WINKLER is a professor at the UCLA School of Law. He is the author of "We the Corporations: How American Businesses Won Their Civil Rights and Gunfight: The Battle Over the Right to Bear Arms in America"

The establishment of "Artificial People" 1886
excerpts with credit to:
https://www.theatlantic.com/business/archive/2018/03/corpora-tions-people-adam-winkler/554852/

A lawyer with decades of practice said to me recently, "you cannot criminally charge a corporation" as we were discussing the public abuses done by banks and investment dealers.
He pointed out that a Corporation is a paper-created entity without a physical body to arrest, handcuff or jail.

Creation of Corporations, artificially derived entities, empowered a new type of surreal person. A person which cannot be confined or controlled. The end game of any uncontrollable-creation is the creation of "giants" and a society which serves these giants, rather than serving humanity. Some parts of society then become eco-nomic slaves to this new kind of monster, while owners of a corpo-ration serve as master. Even though there may be no chains used, the debt costs, living costs, wages or work required to survive, forms invisible economic chains upon society.
As I was writing this, the name of Southern Pacific Railroad rang a bell for some reason. Then I remembered news stories, in Octo-ber 2019, about Pacific Gas and Electric (PGE). PGE was shut-

ting off power to millions of people in California, while the state was hit with rampant fires.

PGE was responsible for some of those fires, due to lack of power line maintenance, while executives and insiders were pillaging the company financially. This is of interest to the overall story since it illustrates the "invisible friend" excuse of corporations.

As executives and shareholders loot the company, to a point where it can no longer maintain it's infrastructure, the loot goes into the pockets of executives and owners. However the public damage comes out of the pockets of PGE's customers and the public. Millions of lives are harmed, some lost by selfish acts of owners and executives. It is free money, with almost zero consequences.

Executives and owners profit from the lawyer-derived belief system which says, "I did not do it, my invisible friend did…"

In related news, as California was on fire, Pacific Gas and Electric obtained bankruptcy protection for itself AND court approval to pay $1/4 billion in executive bonus's.

The Mercury News PG&E gets court OK for $235 million in...

Karl Mondon/Bay Area News Group
PG&E transmission towers in a scorched Butte County forest, November 2018. PG&E will be able to grant $235 million in bonuses roughly 10,000 employees, a bankruptcy judge ruled Tuesday, a decision that was issued despite PG&E's wildfire-linked woes and the disgraced company's proposal to impose a big increase in monthly utility bills on its customers.

The smallest number of humans (one in a million perhaps) control or influence the biggest "creatures" on the planet, political, financial, legal machines, and systems.

Those giant machines are then used to farm the majority of humanity on the planet. This puts most of the world under the yoke of the machines and systems controlled by a few men who have rigged the game.

Should humanity be forced to live with such unfairness? Are systems even legitimate if they are intentionally designed to be unfair to society? Should an artificially created entity be entitled to exist when it allows 0.001% of humans, to farm the rest? Should humanity be forced into a desperate race to deplete the planet in order to survive in such a rigged game? Don't ask a corporate lawyer that question, they will have their own particular "take" on it.

Adam Winkler is a professor of constitutional law at the UCLA School of Law. He is the author of Gunfight: The Battle over the Right to Bear Arms in America, and a commentator about legal issues. Wikipedia

Chapter 9   1913

Federal Reserve Creation

This Chapter is about: A private game of money creation which secretly "borrowed" on the credit backing of the public. This is Trick # 7 for Farming Humans.

It is important because: The banks who print the money, win the game…while the unknowing public both backs the game *and* pays all the costs for the game.

If you gained the franchise to print all the money for everyone in your country, forever, how would that look 100 years later? Recall that President Lincoln created money for free, issued by the government itself. But rich bankers had a better idea…for themselves, not for the country.

Around 1913, a handful of the richest bankers in the world convinced politicians to give these men the franchise to create all US currency. They took America's most valuable public "asset" and privatized it for their own personal benefit.

There is a wealth of information written on the creation of the US Federal Reserve (The "Fed"), so I won't try to replace it here. I just wish to shine some light into man-made belief systems which create the corrupt conditions to farm humans.

The Fed is another non-human entity, invented by bankers, to mostly benefit bankers, and it is perhaps the greatest (non-military) power on the planet.
Readers can check out some videos online to gain their own better understanding.

One example to perhaps start with is this three minute video:
At 02:15 of video: "The Federal Reserve Act of 1913 created 12 districts across the US and established a regional central bank for each district."

> *"These would serve as "banker's banks" for each district."*
> *https://www.youtube.com/watch?v=RfFcNGikROk*

The creation of the Fed was, and still is today, cloaked in mystery.

In point form to simplify things, it went something like this:

1. In the late 1800's, America did not have a strong central bank, and instead had multiple state and private banks competing, taking deposits and issuing promissory notes and currency. Many of these banks did not survive and Americans were often at risk of a new bank panic, and loss of all their money.

2. A solution was needed to create currency stability, in order for America to grow and prosper.

3. The wealthiest financiers of the time, met in 1910 covertly at a private hunting estate on Jekyl Island, just off the coast of Georgia, to come up with a solution.

4. This story is covered quite well in THE CREATURE FROM JEKYL ISLAND, and other good works. I will leave it to readers to research and come to their own conclusions.

5. These wealthy men, proposed to form a private Central Bank, separate from the confines of the US government. An entity owned and controlled by these rich men.

6. This Central Bank would be called the "Federal Reserve", to lend it credibility and public respect, despite it being a private, banker-owned entity.

7. The Federal Reserve would serve two purposes. First it would grant these private owners a sole monopoly on money creation in the US.
   Second, and of benefit to public, it would provide stable funding for the expanding operations of the US government, with this self-created money. It just needed someone to pay all the costs.

8. The money would be "created" out of thin air by the entity born on Jekyl Island, the new Federal reserve, which is perhaps the greatest trick or illusion in the world.

9. To give this paper money credibility and trust, the money would be backed by the full faith and trust of the US Treasury. American taxpayers thus provide the public backing and strength, while private bankers pocket the benefits.

10. Instead of government issuing money itself, like Lincoln did, this private group wanted to bury the public in debt, so banks could gain a permanent income for life from the interest payments, without having to work for it.

11. These bankers proposed that the government give them US Treasury notes, (which the government creates out of thin air) ...and the bankers will give them back money to run the nation, money which the banks created out of thin air.

12. Creating money out of thin air, to trade for government treasury notes created out of thin air, did nothing more than Lincoln's approach of simply issuing the money by government itself...but it did add in a way for the bankers to pocket millions, billions or trillions in interest payments from the US Treasury on the treasury notes created.

13. Critics today point out that Lincoln accomplished much the same thing, without bankers collecting interest in the middle. Perhaps that is one possible reason for someone to want to assassinate President Lincoln.

14. To give a "Payday Lending" comparison, the US population was to be burdened with paying a new personal income tax, used to fund interest payments to the bankers, forever more. Permanent chains of debt now lay upon the American public for every dollar ever created, and a tax was required to make sure bankers got paid the interest on this debt.

If one compares this, with President Lincoln's model of money creation, without using borrowed money from bankers, it is seen that private bankers finally succeeded in their secret work to entrap America in perpetual debt. They used something which rightfully belonged to the US taxpayer, to trap the country into something which enriches private bankers.

========

It appears that the "Fed" was a template for a modern Payday Lending store, and the American public was duped into becoming victims of a permanent debt and tax scheme. I could be wrong, but the similarities are startling. I hope readers will question this and start asking their own questions on how this process works. I claim no particular doorway to the truth in this area where secrecy and confusion are the weapons of financial war.

The Payday lending comparison looks like this in my mind:

1. Each dollar the Fed creates earns them a dividend. It can be as high as 6%, and today it sits at around the 2% mark. (see info box on following page, "**Section 7. Division of Earnings**")

2. Each dollar the Fed creates is created out of thin air. (from nothing)

3. Each dollar created gains its trust and credibility by being backed by promises (IOU's, Treasury Bills, notes or bonds) issued by the US Government.

4. Each dollar the Fed creates thus creates a dollar of _debt placed upon the backs of the U.S. citizens_. (even when the money is loaned or given away in "bailouts" to the same banks which own the Fed…ponder that for a moment)

Try to wrap your mind around a private entity, which creates Trillions of dollars out of nothing but air, diverts Trillions to itself in low cost loans or bailouts, and design it so that every dollar is a debt backed by American taxpayers and not upon those who take the greatest benefit.

I trust that some who read this will explore further and deeper than I am capable of, and that society will benefit from every insight discovered. It is either that, or we continue to let bankers farm humans and create an ever more distressed and fragile society.

Section 7. Division of Earnings
(a) Dividends And Surplus Funds Of Reserve Banks.
1. Stockholder Dividends.
- Dividend Amount. After all necessary expenses of a Federal reserve bank have been paid or provided for, the stockholders of the bank shall be entitled to receive an annual dividend on paid-in capital stock of--
  - in the case of a stockholder with total consolidated assets of more than $10,000,000,000, **the smaller of**--
    - the rate equal to the high yield of the **10-year Treasury note** auctioned at the last auction held prior to the payment of such dividend; **and**
    - **6 percent**; and
  - in the case of a stockholder with total consolidated assets of $10,000,000,000 or less, 6 percent.

Source:
https://www.federalreserve.gov/aboutthefed/section7.htm

So Fed Bankers are:

1. Making Billions by printing or creating society's money.
2. Making more by using each Fed member's private banks to create/lend up to ten times more. (fractional reserve lending)
3. Making immense amounts when projects like war are financed.
4. Making more again by gambling in investment markets.
5. Getting their losses back when banks gambling losses are bailed out by the taxpayer.
6. Making more from the Trillions printed/created to bail out their losses
7. While all this money-making is going on, each and every dollar must be paid back, using the blood, sweat and tears of the American people.
8. Banks seem to get 90% of the benefits, while the American taxpayers pay...forever.
9. Is this what farming humans looks like? A secret billionaire's picnic at public expense?

10. I would be grateful to be corrected on these or other points in this book, since it is not my intention to spread false information, but rather to discover truth in the public interest.

"There is no free lunch and there are no free dollars."
(anon)

Correction, there may be free dollars, but only to the Fed and the private banks who control the Fed. Everyone else is on the hook for paying the debts they create. The more debt, the richer the bankers…(while society becomes poorer).

Certainly the USA has benefitted from the stable currency and robust economy that resulted from establishment of the Fed, but it did not do so in a fair manner, when compared to the Trillions funnelled to bankers. The public benefitted yes, but the public interest was (and still is) cheated horribly in my view.

The Fed, was established by private bankers who secured a "franchise" from government. They have been able to profit from and control entire countries with the power they obtained. (See also "Rentier")

I believe that the Central bank should be a public body of benefit to every single American, and not just a few privately owned entities. It could be converted to that model as easily as it was created. Secondly, if the Government issues debt promises to back each dollar the Fed creates, the government could just as easily back those dollars directly and skip the (Fed) middleman. John Kennedy was yet another U.S. president who saw this logic…and then never saw the completion of his term.

==========

"What does history tell us about functions of Central Banks?"

The first thing we learn is that these were NOT formed to regulate money supply. In fact, the original purpose of creation of Central Banks was to provide funding for wars. For more details, Origins of Central Banking*. Central Banks were created as to provide loans to the State on easy terms, often to finance wars or colonization. They were quite GOOD at this function. Historian Peter Kennedy in his Rise and Fall of Great Powers argues that ability to finance wars was the source of power. Noting the efficiency of Central Banks at providing finance led to widespread imitation, and creation of Central Banks all over Europe.

https://weapedagogy.wordpress.com/2020/04/21/rg2-goodhart-on-central-banks/

*Origins of Central Banking   https://weapedagogy.wordpress.-com/2019/03/31/origins-of-central-banking/

The following excerpt is from an article by Alan Adaschik Guest writer for Wake Up World, titled The Trap of Debt-Based Economics

https://wakeup-world.com/2015/10/24/the-trap-of-debt-economics/?fbclid=IwAR3Xg0ktRqE7F_jNc2CttBg4MdY_2KXdsr-UeceWKrGJL_MzXInQwh0PVbTk

Think about what this has cost the citizens of this nation. If in 1913 the members of Congress did their jobs properly and honored their sacred oath of office, this nation would still be a Republic. Furthermore, with Congress coining our money and regulating its value, there would be no need for an income tax. Governments at all levels would be able to fund everything they do solely out of the wealth realized from establishing credit and loaning money. Taxes would be eliminated and once again Americans would be able to enjoy all the fruits of their labor. Recessions and depressions would be eliminated and only one member of a household would have to work. People would be able to save money and consumer credit would be almost non-existent. The work week and work day would be shorter than they are today and people would be able to take extended vacations. They would also be able to retire earlier in life. All of this would be the status quo for Americans if it were

> *not for the fact that, in 1913, Congress sold us into bondage. Hasn't the time come for Congress to rectify their ignoble and horrible mistake?*

Please do not take my word, or my "mis-understandings" for any of this. What follows are six pages of quotes about the Federal Reserve Bank and The Bank of England which it was modeled upon. Read for yourself what the most well-informed voices said at the time.

From:
http://www.lovethetruth.com/government/federal_reserve/quotes.htm

The Rothschilds
   "The few who understand the system, will either be so interested from it's profits or so dependant on it's favors, that there will be no opposition from that class." — <u>Rothschild Brothers of London, 1863</u>

   "Give me control of a nation's money and I care not who makes it's laws" — <u>Mayer Amschel Bauer Rothschild</u>

Senators and Congressmen
   "Most Americans have no real understanding of the operation of the international money lenders. The accounts of the Federal Reserve System have never been audited. It operates outside the control of Congress and manipulates the credit of the United States" — <u>Sen. Barry Goldwater (Rep. AR)</u>

   "This [Federal Reserve Act] establishes the most gigantic trust on earth. When the President [Wilson} signs this bill, the invisible government of the monetary power will be legalized....the worst legislative crime of the ages is perpetrated by this banking and currency bill." — <u>Charles A. Lindbergh, Sr. , 1913</u>

"The financial system has been turned over to the Federal Reserve Board. That Board as ministers the finance system by authority of a purely profiteering group. The system is Private, conducted for the sole purpose of obtaining the greatest possible profits from the use of other people's money" -- Charles A. Lindbergh Sr., 1923

"The Federal Reserve bank buys government bonds without one penny..." — Congressman
Wright Patman, Congressional Record, Sept 30, 1941

"We have, in this country, one of the most corrupt institutions the world has ever known. I refer to the Federal Reserve Board. This evil institution has impoverished the people of the United States and has practically bankrupted our government. It has done this through the corrupt practices of the moneyed vultures who control it". — Congressman Louis T. McFadden in 1932 (Rep. Pa)

*"The Federal Reserve banks are one of the most corrupt institutions the world has ever seen.
There is not a man within the sound of my voice who does not know that this nation is run by the international bankers".* — Congressman Louis T. McFadden (Rep. Pa)

*"Some people think the Federal Reserve Banks are the United States government's institutions.
They are not government institutions. They are private credit monopolies which prey upon the people of the United States for the benefit of themselves and their foreign swindlers"* — Congressional Record 12595-12603 — Louis T. McFadden, Chairman of the Committee on Banking and Currency (12 years) June 10, 1932

Deep down in our heart, we know that we have given our children a legacy of bankruptcy. We have defrauded our country to get ourselves elected." — <u>John Danforth (R-Mo)</u>

"These 12 corporations together cover the whole country and monopolize and use for private
gain every dollar of the public currency..." — Mr. Crozier of Cincinnati, Senate Banking and Currency Committee - 1913

"The [Federal Reserve Act] as it stands seems to me to open the way to a vast inflation of the currency... I do not like to think that any law can be passed that will make it possible to submerge the gold standard in a flood of irredeemable paper currency." — <u>Henry Cabot Lodge Sr., 1913</u>

From the Federal Reserves Own Admissions
"When you or I write a check there must be sufficient funds in out account to cover the check, but when the Federal Reserve writes a check there is no bank deposit on which that check is drawn. When the Federal Reserve writes a check, it is creating money." — <u>Putting it simply, Boston Federal Reserve Bank</u>

"Neither paper currency nor deposits have value as commodities, intrinsically, a 'dollar' bill is just a piece of paper. Deposits are merely book entries." — <u>Modern Money Mechanics Workbook, Federal Reserve Bank of Chicago, 1975</u>

"We are completely dependent on the commercial banks. Someone has to borrow every dollar we have in circulation, cash or credit. If the banks create ample synthetic money we are prosperous; if not, we starve. We are absolutely without a permanent money system.... It is the most important subject intelligent persons can investigate and reflect upon. It is so important that our present civilization may collapse unless it becomes widely understood and the defects remedied very soon." — <u>Robert H. Hamphill, Atlanta Federal Reserve Bank</u>

"The regional Federal Reserve banks are not government agencies. ...but are independent,
privately owned and locally controlled corporations." — <u>Lewis vs. United States, 680 F. 2d 1239 9th Circuit 1982</u>

Past Presidents, not including the Founding Fathers

"A great industrial nation is controlled by it's system of credit. Our system of credit is concentrated in the hands of a few men. We have come to be one of the worst ruled, one of the most completely controlled and dominated governments in the world--no longer a government of free opinion, no longer a government by conviction and vote of the majority, but a government by the opinion and duress of small groups of dominant men." — <u>President Woodrow Wilson</u>

"I believe that banking institutions are more dangerous to our liberties than standing armies. Already they have raised up a monied aristocracy that has set the government at defiance. The issuing power (of money) should be taken away from the banks and restored to the people to whom it properly belongs." — <u>Thomas Jefferson, U.S. President.</u>

"History records that the money changers have used every form of abuse, intrigue, deceit, and violent means possible to maintain their control over governments by controlling money and it's issuance." — <u>James Madison</u>

"It is well that the people of the nation do not understand our banking and monetary system, for if they did, I believe there would be a revolution before tomorrow morning." — <u>Henry Ford</u>

"...the increase in the assets of the Federal Reserve banks from 143 million dollars in 1913 to 45 billion dollars in 1949 went directly to the private stockholders of the [federal reserve] banks." —

Eustace Mullins

"The modern Banking system manufactures money out of nothing. The process is perhaps the most astounding piece of sleight of hand that was ever invented. Banks can in fact inflate, mint and un-mint the modern ledger-entry currency." — MAJOR L .L. B. ANGUS:

"While boasting of our noble deeds were careful to conceal the ugly fact that by an iniquitous money system we have nationalized a system of oppression which, though more refined, is no less cruel than the old system of chattel slavery. — Horace Greeley

"It is absurd to say our Country can issue bonds and cannot issue currency. Both are promises to pay, but one fattens the usurer and the other helps the People. If the currency issued by the People were no good, then the bonds would be no good, either. It is a terrible situation when the Government, to insure the National Wealth, must go in debt and submit to ruinous interest charges at the hands of men who control the fictitious value of gold. Interest is the invention of Satan." — THOMAS A. EDISON

"By this means government may secretly and unobserved, confiscate the wealth of the people, and not one man in a million will detect the theft." — John Maynard Keynes (the father of 'Keynesian Economics' which our nation now endures) in his book "THE ECONOMIC CONSEQUENCES
OF THE PEACE" (1920).

"Most Americans have no real understanding of the operation of the international money lenders. The accounts of the Federal Reserve System have never been audited. It operates outside the control of Congress and manipulates the credit of the United States" — Senator Barry Goldwater (Rep. AR)

"Whoever controls the volume of money in any country is absolute master of all industry and commerce."
— James A. Garfield President of the United States

"100 Years Is Enough: Time to Make the Fed a Public Utility"
— Ziad K. Abdelnour

I believe that the market is slowly waking up to the fact that the Federal Reserve is a clueless organization. They have no idea what they're doing. And so the confidence level of investors is diminishing, in my view. Marc Faber

When I did my research on this topic, I came to the startling conclusion that the Federal Reserve System does not need to be audited - it needs to be abolished. G. Edward Griffin

Woodrow Wilson would regret his actions and before his death, stated: "*I am a most unhappy man--unwittingly I have ruined my country.*" The bill passed on December 22, 1913, and President Wilson signed it into law the next day.

"It is no coincidence that the century of total war coincided with the century of central banking."
— Ron Paul

http://www.lovethetruth.com/government/federal_reserve/quotes.htm Ch 9

Chapter 10 1913
Federal Income Tax Creation

This Chapter is about: How Americans were forced (tricked?) into paying income taxes, as the foundation for Billions in profits for private bankers. (Farming Humans trick #7 continued)

It is important because: It again illustrates the Payday Lending analogy that American taxpayers are burdened with and makes one wonder how much unjust enrichment those private bankers earned, or owe to the American public.

The Revenue Act of 1913, also known as the Underwood Tariff or the Underwood-Simmons Act (ch. 16, 38 Stat. 114), re-established a federal income tax in the United States and lowered tariff rates. The act was sponsored by Representative Oscar Underwood, passed by the 63rd United States Congress, and signed into law by President Woodrow Wilson.

History Brief: The Federal Income Tax and the Federal Reserve
3 min video
https://www.youtube.com/watch?v=RfFcNGikROk

"The Revenue Act of 1913 was signed into law, and the bill, also known as the Underwood Act, is considered a major triumph for President Wilson.
The Sixteenth Amendment, ratified in 1913, legalized the use of an income tax.
This new tax would generate funding for the federal government by taxing corporate profits and the individual earnings of US citizens.
By 1917, the federal government was receiving more revenue from the income tax than tariffs had ever brought in.
Today, income and corporate taxes represent the bulk of the federal government's funding."
Wikipedia

So, at this point, one can imagine a simple structure where the U.S. Treasury needs truckloads of money to expand and develop the country into the powerhouse that it will become. A private group of wealthy men convince the politicians of the day that they can provide this money, by leaning upon the borrowing power of the US government, if this unique franchise is granted to them.

The US government will issue promissory notes (IOU's, treasury bills, bonds etc) to the Federal Reserve (the "Fed"). Each is backed by a repayment promise from the US government and is a public borrowing which must be paid back. The Fed adds these notes, treasury bills, etc, onto their books, making the Fed look instantly like it is worth millions, billions or trillions, in government assets, notes, bonds and bills.

In return, the Fed creates banknotes or digital currency out of nothing, using the US government IOU's as the "security", "backing" or "promise" behind this money. There may have been some government (or Fed) owned gold that factored into the equation, but I am unclear on this and I need to learn more.

The new Fed "created" money gets deposited into government bank accounts at a number of Fed-related banks around the country. These giant money deposits into banks owned by the same bankers who own the Fed, gives the bankers an endless stream of deposits that they can then also lend out. Using fractional reserve lending, the private Fed-related banks are able to lend up to ten times the amount of dollars on deposit. If a trillion dollars were in their banks, they can "create" and lend another ten trillion dollars...are you seeing a second pattern of free money creation yet?

Obtaining this private privilege (free money at public expense) might be something the American people might wish to "re-negotiate" at some time, to restore this valuable public asset to its place of benefit to the American public.

Fractional Reserve
The Federal Reserve requires banks and other depository institu-
tions to hold a minimum level of reserves against their liabilities.
Currently, the marginal reserve requirement equals 10 percent of a
bank's demand and checking deposits.

https://www.newyorkfed.org/research/epr/02v08n1/0205benn/
0205benn.html
If I am making this clear, you may have noted that this appears
designed to create a safe, respected, and trusted money on which
to build an empire. One based on a government guarantee, and a
powerful group of rich men. The rich men found a way to "borrow"
both the credit and the credibility of the U.S., and to create pros-
perity and confidence in the country out of promises and thin air. I
must admit that I give it my respect in it's design, and I recognize
that it created one of the most flourishing economies on earth. It
would be perfect except for the bankers taking advantage of the
government, and the financial interests of the American people.

In the ensuing 100 years of fog and secrecy, the details may have
not been told to the American public. If you are a financial systems detective you will point out that the dozen or so rich men,
have placed themselves and their banks at the front of the line for
the fees upon fees, benefits, and perhaps even some of this freely
created money. (See "Cantillon effect" about those at the "front
of the line" for freshly minted money)

The **Cantillon Effect** refers to the change in prices resulting from
a change in money supply. The change in prices occurs because
the change in money supply has a specific injection (entry) point.

Newly printed money goes to Fed member banks first.
These banks get the "wholesale" cost, and can then use fractional
reserve money creation to create more money freely.
This creates a class of persons who are first in line for billions or
trillions of free or low-interest dollars, while the remainder of the
world must pay retail rates of interest, which requires human
blood, sweat and tears. This insider class wins…by clever design.

See "Fractional Reserve Banking Explained in One Minute" on Youtube for a 60 second tutorial on how a $1000 bank deposit can be turned into $10,000 using fractional reserve banking. It is yet another method which allows creation of money out of thin air.

https://www.youtube.com/watch?v=-09ap6zlB6l

How long would it take you to own 80% of planet earth, if you had this "front of the line" status for low cost or zero cost money? It is little more complex than a crooked Monopoly game where the player who acts as the banker, prints money for himself, buys any property he wishes and charges rent to the other players to pay for it all.

Recall a page or two back that using something called fractional reserve lending, banks are able to lend (create from nothing) up to ten times the amount of dollars they hold on deposit, and the money they show on deposit is created by the Fed itself out of nothing but thin air.

This may be a foundational flaw (or self-serving feature:) of the Fed which appears to create intentional unfairness for the American public, and is a private gift to bankers.

If a small group of men can create money out of nothing, and the rest of society cannot do the same without going to jail, this results in a society where one group can soon own almost everything, while many of the rest must work like slaves, to own anything, or even to survive in such a game. That unfairness is something which is evident in today's (2020) society.

It is an example of repealing the laws of poverty, but just for people of influence. Just 237 years ago, America fought the British to escape the concept of being "farmed" by them. The fight for fairness and equality is seen in "We hold these truths to be self-evident: that all men are created equal". The once greatest nation on earth may have been built on a foundation of men being equal, but for the last 120 years, some clever men have made themselves "much more equal than others".

The greater magic, if such a thing is possible, and the most amazing trick upon the public, was to find a way to pay back the treasury obligations, to pay the interest costs, and to give serious credibility to "where is the money coming from to pay for all our free money"? The bankers had a way in mind...the Revenue Act of 1913.

This was revealed to me long after wondering how the magic machine truly worked. Like others, I found the Fed story interesting, intriguing, complex, and not well explained. Instead it seemed disguised in jargon and language resembling the priests of old who spoke in Latin. I became resigned to never understand it, until some dots finally connected, and an image of the illusion fell into place. The connection was from what is now seen on every other commercial block in my city, the payday lending shops who prey upon financial illiterates and the vulnerable. Imagine how much money you could put into your own pockets if you designed a financial system where an entire population was kept financially illiterate…and stuck in perpetual debt? Farming Humans and payday lending share some of the same tricks.

When I realized the timing of the Federal Income Tax Act of 1913, it began looking like the dream solution of any payday lending store, as a way to harvest money from the masses. The dots finally connected.

The Fed could create any amount of money out of virtually nothing but thin air and US backed credibility. All they needed was "someone" to pay-back the debt that was used to "back" the money. That someone was the American people. It is a shame (and perhaps a crime) that the American people get the bill, while private banks get most of the benefits. But then, most will never know.

I was watching YouTube videos, trying to find more about how the money machine worked when I ran across a speaker that simplified it to a level that even I could understand.

A set of videos by Mike Maloney brought the Fed into clearer focus. There are hundreds of good speakers, and the job of a financial nerd is to sort through and try to separate the real from the false. I found Mike Maloney to offer a good balance of facts and clarity.

The "Hidden Secrets of Money" is one of his works that I think should be shown to students in high school, to teach them financial literacy, as well as financial system literacy. This is not taught, or when it is, the teaching is usually tainted by quid pro quo's from a highly conflicted financial industry. Sadly, those folks are more interested in making sure that the public never gets an understanding of financial literacy.

Agnotologist tip: *Less-informed people are easier to take advantage of financially.*

One video by Mike Maloney connected a half dozen dots for me and is worth mention. It is titled "Decoding The Elite Plan For The World Economy - Mike Maloney On Federal Reserve Strategy".

I know that is a mouthful, and yes, it contains enough information that perhaps only financial nerds would watch it. However it also contains a clear and simple breakdown of jargon and Fed-speak. Fed-speak is the language that is designed to make people throw up their arms and say, "I cannot understand any of this stuff, I give up." (this is the same "complication con", that false investment "advisors", and Latin-speaking priests use to dupe the public)

Giving up and not understanding the foundations of money is an easy out, and is also the way to be farmed. By making it complicated, 99% of humans mentally detach. It makes cheating them as easy as taking candy from a baby, except the candy is the wealth in a nation, and the baby is 99% of humans in the nation, or on the planet.

When humans are kept financially dumbed down, they have no choice but to believe what the priests of money tell them is right… right?

Financial literacy and systemic literacy is a bit like the invention of the printing press, in Martin Luther's time, pre 1500. It means that no longer do we have to believe the self serving jargon sold by the high priests of money, We can now try to understand it ourselves, and use that knowledge to benefit society. That is one of the trillion-dollar solutions that this book imagines, and I believe it could change the world.

Mike Maloney's video shone a light upon not only the actions of the Federal Reserve, but on the complex language that they use to conceal and hide their actions. Watching Mike Maloney make it simple, twigged my Agnotologist mind to finally realize that what the Fed does is not complicated, they just intentionally make it sound like Greek so the public never attempts to even see the simple crimes.

Mr. Maloney walks the audience through what each word, phrase or concept means. He explains it with an intent to help people to understand, rather than to confuse.

I found a new understanding that helped me to put the Fed in its proper place in my mind. It's all about how to farm humans, by learning how to financially harm humans, by first knowing how to confuse humans, and politicians.

I also discovered another important trick (among many in this video).

That trick was in *never telling* the American people that *they had to pay for it, and that they would be paying interest to the bankers…forever.* They hide the payday-lending "ruse" from the people, and our "trusted" Fed continues to fool 99.999% of people today.

The 16th amendment, ratified in 1913, legalized the use of an income tax upon every income earner in the country.

Prior to this the government existed upon occasional estate taxes, and corporate income taxes which began in 1909. It was a time when American men and women were truly free to live, work and exist as they wished. It truly was the land of the free…for a little while. I am told that a man could support his family and provide a roof over their heads by working about three months per year.

Today, many families cannot survive on two or more working incomes. This taxation burden on society is another indicator of 100 years of systemic farming of a society, especially so when many of the largest income earners now find ways to avoid paying taxes.

Imagine the human freedom possible if there were no personal taxes upon people, and instead the government were supported by taxes upon corporations? Upon those "artificial" persons, the ones who cannot be arrested, handcuffed or jailed. Instead of government doing the dirty political work of making corporations more profitable, while humans and the planet suffers, it could just as simply be turned on its head. Today the corporations escape, avoid or evade billions in taxes, and ordinary people have no means of escape. Those people are now treated more like slaves, to corporate and government masters. (The servants have taken over the mansion, both politically and financially.)

"The plethora of taxes we pay today – federal income tax, alternative minimum tax, corporate tax, estate tax, FICA, and so on – didn't always exist. America's first citizens enjoyed few to no taxes, and taxes were added, increased and occasionally (and often temporarily) repealed to give us the current tax regime. Let's explore the origins of some of the more common taxes we face today."

"The federal income tax was enacted in 1913, and corporate income taxes were enacted slightly earlier, in 1909."

Quotations from AMY FONTINELLE, writing for Investopedia
https://www.investopedia.com/articles/tax/10/history-taxes.asp

A cynic, looking back on 100+ years of history, seeing the economic hardship of many North Americans today, might see a connection in those two things that occurred in 1913-1914. The creation of the Federal Reserve to print money, and the income tax to pay for it…without end.

Was the Fed, plus the income tax, the first "payday lending" financial model? Support each printed dollar with taxpayer-owed debt, (US Treasury notes) and then collect taxes to pay back parts of the debt…forever.

With the economic borrowing power of the USA based upon the labor of millions of working Americans, should the greatest financial benefits, go to a handful of private bankers who outsmarted everyone? If the system is not fair for America, is it even legitimate? If not legitimate, should Americans stand up for it? Should young Americans be asked to die for it?

Are all wars really Bankers wars, as has been claimed?
I believe the private bankers who created the Federal Reserve have obtained public and private personal benefits, and that those benefits rightly belong to the American public. Some U.S. presidents who discovered this concept have met with an untimely end, so perhaps it is also time to end this chapter.

Search "All wars are bankers wars", on YouTube to learn more.

Chapter 11 1929
Women become "persons" in Canada

This Chapter is about: More silly man-made systems for humans to believe.

It is important because: It shines light into the sometimes silly and often self-serving nature of our man made belief systems.

As we get to 1929, women are finally considered to be persons, about 30 years behind Corporations being granted this in Canada or the U.S.

Imagine a society where corporations were recognized as persons, *before the only persons who can literally create persons,...are considered persons.* That is key indicator of an unfairly rigged game, or a bad belief system.

Universal suffrage.

The concept of universal franchise, also known as general suffrage or common suffrage of the common man, consists of the right to vote for all adult citizens, regardless of wealth, income, gender, social status, race, or ethnicity, subject only to minor exceptions. Wikipedia

1929: **Women become persons**. On Oct. 18, 1929, women are finally declared "persons" under Canadian law.

The historic legal victory is due to the persistence of five Alberta women -- Emily Murphy, Nellie McClung, Irene Parlby, Louise McKinney and Henrietta Muir Edwards. The battle started in 1916. From Murphy's very first day as a judge, lawyers had challenged her rulings because she is not a "person" under Canadian law.

By 1927, the women have garnered support all across Canada. They petition the nation's Supreme Court. After five weeks of debate, the appeal is unanimously denied. Shocked, the women take the fight to the Privy Council of the British government; in those days it was Canada's highest court. In this CBC Radio clip from June 11, 1938, Prime Minister William Lyon Mackenzie King un-

veils a plaque commemorating the women activists in what became known as the "Persons Case" and Nellie McClung, one of
two surviving members of the "Famous Five," speaks of the historic struggle.
https://www.cbc.ca/archives/entry/1929-women-become-persons

Timeline of women's legal rights in the United States

The Cable Act of 1922 (ch. 411, 42 Stat. 1021, "Married Women's
Independent Nationality Act") was a United States federal law that
reversed former immigration laws regarding marriage. (It is also
known as the Married Women's Citizenship Act or the Women's
Citizenship Act).
Other short titles: Married Women's Citizenship ...
Long title: An Act relative to the naturalization ...
Acts repealed: Expatriation Act of 1907
Titles amended: 8 U.S.C.: Aliens and Nationality

Cable Act - Wikipedia

Women's rights seem more complicated and manipulated than the
financial markets, so I had better just leave this topic quickly before my ignorance is proven beyond all doubt. It is here simply to
reinforce the idea that strange men do strange things with power.
It is all connected to the topic of how to farm humans.

Chapter 12   1933

FDR signs the Glass-Steagall Act, separating banks from investment banks.

This Chapter is about: A protective step taken after the 1929 market crash, to separate banks and investment banking or speculating.

It is important because: It provided safety for financial systems until this act was repealed by Bill Clinton in 1999, opening the world to our coming 21st century economic depressions.

By 1933 many felt that the stock market crash of 1929, and Great Depression of the 1930's were caused by banks who were gambling in markets with depositors money that should be kept away from high risk activity. The Glass Steagall Act was intended to bring separation between banking and investment activities.

BY REEM HEAKAL
In 1933, in the wake of the 1929 stock market crash and during a nationwide commercial bank failure and the Great Depression, two members of Congress put their names on what is known today as the Glass-Steagall Act (GSA). This act separated investment and commercial banking activities. At the time, "improper banking activity," or what was considered overzealous commercial bank involvement in stock market investment, was deemed the main culprit of the financial crash. According to that reasoning, commercial banks took on too much risk with depositors' money. Additional, and sometimes non-related, explanations for the Great Depression evolved over the years, and many questioned whether the GSA hindered the establishment of financial services firms that can equally compete against each other.
BY REEM HEAKAL of Investopedia

It is worth mentioning why the Glass Steagall Act was important to your family, mine, and to the farming of humans. If banks have ways to create free or nearly free money from the printing process, and from fractional reserve lending, and IF they decide to gamble with that money, they become very rich from their winnings. But what happens to the losses? There is zero incentive to not "bet it all", if banks can count on naive or corrupt systems to bail them out of their losses.

In a world where banks are "too big to fail", and also can lose so much money that the country, or the global financial system is at risk of collapse, then the government (taxpayers) must be "used" to forgive them their debts and their mistakes. It is like a Debt Jubilee for gambling addicts...repeat as often needed, while society pays for it.

Chapter 13   1933

Public Gold Confiscated

This Chapter is about: The repeal of the tangible gold backing behind each U.S. dollar, changing the backing and the substance behind money itself.

It is important because: It marks a step from having some limits on money creation, to limitless money creation.

In March 1933, the Federal Reserve Bank of New York chose to no longer honor its commitment to convert currency to gold for U.S. citizens. President Franklin Roosevelt declared a national banking holiday.

A run on gold reserves caused President Roosevelt to close banks. Banks reopen after relinquishing all gold to the Federal Reserve. Roosevelt orders Americans to turn gold in for dollars, which creates gold reserves at Fort Knox.

Executive Order 6102 is a United States presidential executive order signed on April 5, 1933, by President Franklin D. Roosevelt "forbidding the hoarding of gold coin, gold bullion, and gold certificates within the continental United States".

POSTMASTER: PLEASE POST IN A CONSPICUOUS PLACE.—JAMES A. FARLEY, Postmaster General

UNDER EXECUTIVE ORDER OF THE PRESIDENT

Issued April 5, 1933

all persons are required to deliver

ON OR BEFORE MAY 1, 1933

all GOLD COIN, GOLD BULLION, AND GOLD CERTIFICATES now owned by them to a Federal Reserve Bank, branch or agency, or to any member bank of the Federal Reserve System.

Executive Order

In 1934 The Gold Reserve Act prohibits <u>private ownership</u> of gold. Roosevelt then increases the price of gold for the first time in 100 years.

Yes, gold as a form of backing money is a belief system, nothing more. We could just as easily use acorns to back our money or as a form of money itself. Or we could use the currency itself, just paper, and say that is good enough. That is essentially what removal of the gold standard for the public accomplished.

However gold did offer important checks and balances, in that it is somewhat rare, cannot be counterfeited, and is difficult to obtain. These qualities created limits on the amount of gold, which created limits on money-printing. Without a gold backing, or a backing of solid, valuable, tangible means, money is just a paper promise and nothing more. It is very easy to cheat with paper promises.

Paper promises can be made in infinite quantity, and so can money without tangible asset limitations. When there are no limits to how much money can be created, and when the Federal Reserve and its member banks get richer by each dollar created, the more the merrier. Lend a trillion dollars and banks make billions. Start a war and make more…much more.

This instills warped incentives into the monetary system and among the banks who own the Fed. Along with private profits to a private entity, other dangers to society are created. First is the temptation to start wars, since starting a war is the fastest way to spend money, it provides the most profitable customer for the banks. The problem is in enemies that must be created, and lives that must be lost, in order to create wars solely for the purpose of lending money.

It is sad to watch such a game. A banker/politician game where the more money they can take using a rigged system, the worse life must become for the society they pretend to serve.

Chapter 14   1944

Bretton Woods Agreement

This Chapter is about: The US Dollar becomes the world reserve currency due to its partial gold-backing.

It is important because: It marks the beginning of global reliance upon one sole monetary-mind, the U.S. Federal Reserve plus a few related central banks. What could go wrong?

Bretton Woods refers to the international monetary arrangement of allied nations in 1944 that created the IMF and World Bank, and that set up a system of fixed exchange rates with the US dollar as the international reserve currency.

The Bretton Woods Conference, officially known as the United Nations Monetary and Financial Conference, brought delegates from 44 nations to Bretton Woods, New Hampshire, to agree upon a series of new rules for the post-WWII international monetary system.

Their aims were to rebuild the shattered postwar economy and to promote international economic cooperation.
The Bretton Woods exchange-rate system saw all currencies linked to the dollar, and the dollar linked to gold. The US was said to hold the largest quantity of gold reserves at the time, and gold was still used as the most consistent measure of financial strength and stability of a country. (Other countries and trading partners were still allowed to convert US dollars to gold, but not private citizens.)

In a side-bar which illustrates why gold (or silver etc) can be used as a reasonable measure of financial strength, take a look at the "Difference between currency and money", in this two minute You-Tube video.Viewers will gain a quick and clear understanding of how currencies are easily devalued when powers can literally "rain money" from the printing presses.

https://www.youtube.com/watch?v=BfSisiYoEEA

While doing the research for this book, I recall running across a story about how Hitler created his economic miracle in Germany, by skirting the bankers and issuing Germany's own sovereign currency backed by the government, and not using bankers loans. I thought at the time that it was an interesting story but I did not want to be side-tracked at that time.

Now I regret not having more knowledge about how that worked. If I recall, the jist of the story was that when a country decides to go it alone, to bypass global financiers for their borrowing or money-creation requirements, bad things tend to happen to the leaders or to those countries.

It could be a coincidence or a conspiracy, but it is something I would be interested in learning more about. The game of money is so multi-dimensional (and usually invisible) that wars and history often include hidden connections to games of money masters. The public, of course, is told of other reasons beside the secret motivations of the masters.

Chapter 15   1971

End of Bretton Woods

End of all gold in the game.
Now it is bits of paper only.
Beginning of "Bubble Backed Currency"
(Bubble Backed means Money backed by nothing)

This Chapter is about: Removal of the gold backing of US dollars for global trading partners, a second default of the promises behind the dollar. Trick #8 in the Farming of Humans.

It is important because: It coincides with beginnings of experiments in "bubble blowing" currency creation by the Fed.

In 1971 the U.S. ended conversion of U.S. dollars into gold. The costs of a 20 year military effort in Vietnam is attributed as one cause, as this war had cost America a great deal more than they ever expected.

The Americans abandoned any hope of victory after 1968. They were just battling to save face. "They know they've got us by the balls," Nixon admitted privately.

The Americans engaged in talks with North Vietnam, but when nothing came of those by 1972, the communists launched another offensive. Nixon retaliated with the heaviest bombing of the war over North Vietnam during May and June 1972.
The Nixon administration quietly offered to pay North Vietnam $10bn in reparations once the fighting stopped. A peace was concluded to end the war in 1974, but nobody doubted the US had lost.

This became blatantly obvious in April 1975, when the communists seized all of Vietnam, and the world witnessed the panic-stricken evacuation from the roof of the US embassy in Saigon.

> *More than 58,000 American troops were killed in Vietnam, along with as many as 3 million Vietnamese. Should anybody have been surprised by the Nixon administration's contempt for democracy? The Americans dropped four times more explosives on North Vietnam during this operation than on Japan during the Second World War. Johnson also increased the number of American troops in Vietnam from 16,000 to 459,500.* Ryle Dwyer, Irish Examiner, November 17, 2018

For half a century beginning in 1879, Americans could turn in $20.67 worth of paper dollars and receive an ounce of gold. The country effectively abandoned the gold standard in 1933, and completely severed the link between the dollar and gold in 1971.

Why did the Bretton Woods system come to an end?

On August 15, 1971, President Richard M. Nixon announced his New Economic Policy, a program "to create a new prosperity without war." Known colloquially as the "Nixon shock," the initiative marked the beginning of the end for the Bretton Woods system.

There is no such thing as a world currency. However, since World War II, the dominant currency of the world had been the U.S. dollar.

Because fiat money (money by decree) is not linked to tangible or physical wealth, it risks losing value due to inflation or even becoming worthless in the event of hyperinflation. If people lose faith in a nation's currency, the money will no longer hold value.

Nixon revoked the Gold Backed Status of the US Dollar after other nations begin asking questions, and requesting gold instead of American paper dollars. After 19 years and 180 days of fighting a seemingly un-winnable war in Vietnam, the country was drained financially to the point of having to close the door upon their greatest strength. Their gold for paper dollars promise.

This was a second "default" for the American dollar. The first being in 1933 for American citizens, and a second now, for international trading partners or countries. The U.S. dollar thus became a "fiat" currency. (It is money by "fiat" only, or money only because someone says it is)

Looking back, 1971 seems to mark a new period of Federal Reserve experiments in unlimited money creation. Now that gold backed limits were off, it allowed the beginning of "blowing bubbles" with paper money.

Removing the gold backing behind US dollars freed the Fed from all limits to the amount of money it could create. Without a tangible gold backing, the US dollar becomes a paper promise. A game of trust. How far can you push a game of trust? How big a bubble can you make?

If the United States returned to the gold standard and then faced an economic crisis, the government would not be permitted to use monetary policy (such as injecting stimulus money into the economy) to avert financial disaster.

Yet the US dollar was still considered a global reserve currency, so even without the gold backing the US dollar still held respect around the globe in 1971. Imagine having the trust of the whole world, and a magic dollar-creation machine…with no limits on it.

Here is a non-academic explanation of what is meant by Blowing Bubbles:

"Blowing bubbles" is a slang term used by those who follow economics and money creation. It describes the childlike ease with which paper-backed money can be created. It is so easy it is like blowing bubbles for a child. However Fed moves to balance or manipulate the economy are done without them knowing all the possible effects. They are trial and error in nature. Finally, the ability to toss billions or trillions of dollars in any direction desired, causes asset price bubbles, (stocks, real estate, etc go up in value) to inflate to unsustainable proportions, before bursting and causing the inevitable bust in the economy.

With the Federal Reserve no longer restrained by gold-backed money limits, it began what appears to be a series of financial experiments to learn how to drive this "new" US monetary vehicle. Allan Greenspan was a Fed Reserve Chairman from 1986 to 2006 and had much to do with the experimenting. As with any new, inexperienced driver, mistakes in judgement are to be expected and crashes happen.

P. J. O'Rourke came closest with the following statement:

"Giving money and power to government is like giving whiskey and car keys to teenage boys."

From Wikipedia, the free encyclopedia

Alan Greenspan (born March 6, 1926) is an American economist who served as Chair of the Federal Reserve of the United States from 1987 to 2006. First appointed Federal Reserve chairman by President Ronald Reagan in August 1987, he was reappointed at successive four-year intervals until retiring on January 31, 2006, after the second-longest tenure in the position (behind William McChesney Martin).[1]

Greenspan came to the Federal Reserve Board from a consulting career. Although he was subdued in his public appearances, favorable media coverage raised his profile to a point that several observers likened him to a "rock star". Democratic leaders of Congress criticized him for politicizing his office because of his support for Social Security privatization and tax cuts, which they felt would increase the deficit.

The easy-money policies of the Fed during Greenspan's tenure have been suggested by some to be a leading cause of the dot-com bubble, and the subprime mortgage crisis (occurring within a year of his leaving the Fed), which, said the Wall Street Journal, "tarnished his reputation." Yale economist Robert Shiller argues that "once stocks fell, real estate became the primary outlet for the speculative frenzy that the stock market had unleashed".

> *Greenspan argues that the housing bubble was not a product of low-interest rates but rather a worldwide phenomenon caused by the precipitous decline in long term interest rates.*

Bubble after bubble (price booms, followed by crash and price-bust) in various sectors of the economy appear as hindsight evidence of unaware men behind the curtains, fiddling with the dials and controls of the world economy, pretending they were wizards. Untrained chimpanzees could appear as wizards if given the ability to 'rain money' upon the world…

Lifestyles of the Rich and Famous 1984

The show, LIFESTYLES OF THE RICH AND FAMOUS with host Robin Leech, gives clues to when the Fed began blowing bubbles. It supports the premise that it may have been the 1971 actions of Nixon administration that began the era of Federal Reserve experimentation into money printing and blowing bubbles.

Lifestyles of the Rich and Famous is an American television series that aired in syndication from 1984 to 1995. The show featured the extravagant **lifestyles** of **wealthy** entertainers, athletes and business moguls. It was hosted by Robin Leach for the majority of its run.

en.wikipedia.org › wiki › Lifestyles_of_the_Rich_and_Famous ▾
Lifestyles of the Rich and Famous - Wikipedia

Bubbles (and crashes) which occurred after 1971

Internet-era Dot-com Bubble and crash (1999, 2000)

Housing and mortgage bubble and crash (2000 to 2008)

Post 2008 crisis (bankers bailed out and Quantitative Easing (money printing) to restore confidence) market bubble 2008 to 2020.
(1920's stock market bubble may have been related to the early drivings of the Fed, but I reserve my interest for those bubbles after 1971, which I believe relate to a no-longer "backed" dollar.

So what is Quantitative Easing anyway? (the short definition is "blowing bubbles" or 'raining money' for those wishing to skip the longer definition below) Again, picture the Wizard of Oz, behind the curtains pulling levers and twisting dials try to make monetary (money supply etc) conditions just right. The Fed does the inputs but they don't control the outcomes once the money enters the economy. They only control who gets the easy-money first. Watching Fed Chairpersons over the years reminds me of taking my children to the local fair and putting them on the tiny-tots car driving ride. At ages three and four none of them understood that they were not actually driving the vehicle. They believed they were in control. Watching them happily manipulate the steering wheel and beep the horn, while going in controlled circles on a track, reminds me of any Fed chairman in action.

Quantitative Easing: The introduction of new money into the money supply by a central bank.

If the term "quantitative easing" is difficult to grasp, think of it like a drug addict calling his act of injecting heroin, "chemical easing".

A more detailed explanation follows below for those who might prefer.

1. Quantitative easing,(QE) also known as large-scale asset purchases, is a monetary policy whereby a central bank prints money to buy government bonds or other financial assets in order to inject money directly into the economy. *The money comes from debt placed upon the American taxpayer, but the stimulus money usually gets given or cheaply lent to bankers who own the Fed, giving banks an advantage over every other sector of society.*

2. Like lowering interest rates, QE stimulates the economy and eases some of the economic difficulties faced. *Like drugs injected by an addict bring the effect of temporarily blotting out his or her mental difficulties for a time.*

3. Since the Federal Reserve creates money out of nothing, (Americans must pay for it) when it chooses to inject money directly into the economy, Quantitative easing (QE) is an indirect method of printing money for free or nearly zero cost to the main beneficiaries.

4. Creating infinite bits of paper, to represent the finite tangible "wealth" of the planet, causes incentives to destroy the tangible wealth of the earth, in a human-race to gather as many colored papers (dollars) as possible. *Many addicts will also seek and destroy to gain their chemical stimulus.*

5. The Fed launched "quantitative easing" (QE), ultimately buying trillions of dollars of government bonds and mortgage-backed securities. Between 2008 and 2015, the Fed printed trillions. During the final four months of 2019 the Fed was printing between 3 trillion and 6 trillion dollars into an overnight, interbank lending market to keep some unknown, unspoken crisis from causing a repeat of the 2008 financial system meltdown. (Then came Covid-19 as this book was in editing) (see https://wallstreetonparade.com for reporting on that process)

6. Every dollar printed is a debt or "dollar-owed" by the US Treasury, which must be repaid by taxpayers. Even if the Fed gives/

lends the printed money to a narrow group of the population, many of whom can avoid or escape paying taxes.

Limitless money creation, equals unlimited fuel for stock markets, jets, yachts, real estate, and private islands, while the true growth engines of the economy and innovation are put in last place for this easy money game. Millions obtain no benefit at all, and are stuck with paying the tax bill. The Fed seems to have a track record of enriching those related to the Fed, instead of serving society fairly as the portrait of the Fed implies.

It has the side effect of adding un-payable debt onto the backs of the American public, and unlimited wealth to the banks. Everyone knows about the prosperity side of the American economic machine, but not everyone is well versed on how each dollar printed by the Fed, is like a very profitable Payday Loan upon the American people. It is only if you ask yourself how there are half a million homeless Americans sleeping on sidewalks and under freeways, does one begin to see the weight of that debt upon real humans. They are not all "weak" or "lazy", but it is just as likely that they are not on the inside of the secret money cartels that seem to run America.

Artificial humans get most of the wealth of the nation, while real humans are forced to pay the bills…if you are not rich enough to own your own bank, or other corporation, then you are sub-human…in a land where all men were once equal.
 Who among us could not become wealthy beyond imagination if we were connected to the money printing machine that can rain money? And who among us could afford to live in a world where Trillions of dollars are raining from the sky, but only upon banks and billionaires who own corporations? That would be like playing a game of Monopoly where at each turn, the banker secretly gives one million dollars to himself, and nothing to the others. Does that make the losers weak?

North America is now lifted, but only by the efforts of an unlimited money creation machine, with nothing but air, confidence and taxpayer debt backing this new money? How long can that money creation game last? How big can you blow a bubble?

How closely does this unfairly rigged financial system, resemble the rigged British system which triggered the American Revolution? "Same shit, different shovel", is what some say.

=========

Around the time that the US was defaulting on the gold backing of its money, (1971) the Central Bank of Canada (and later France, and perhaps others unknown to me) were apparently forbidden from issuing interest free loans for things like roads, bridges, canals, universities and other essential infrastructure, including education, healthcare, and social services.

Instead these governments were required to start borrowing from private commercial banks to conduct what they previously could do for free. We begin to see the newfound global influence and takeover of government activity of BIS, Bank of International settlements (based in Basel, Switzerland) and related non-government global financial cartels. I could be wrong, but the tracks are there, despite being rather well obscured and difficult to follow.

A class action lawsuit linked below, (which did not obtain permission to proceed in Canada) claims that the removal of the Bank of Canada's right to issue interest free debt for the benefit of public interest projects, caused Canada to be forced into borrowing from private bankers instead. Borrowing from private bankers has cost Canada approximately $1.1 Trillion in interest costs, as of 2015 according to case documents.

The legal case is a look at how easily nation's financial systems can be taken over by cabals of private banking interests. I recommend it for anyone interested in well researched descriptions of how to financially farm humans.
see http://www.comer.org/content/AmendedClaimStatement26-Mar2015.pdf

A Yellow Vests Protester in France (2019) also spoke of the frustration of having their French Central Bank neutered:

"Ever since France became part of Europe, it lost all its national sovereignty, it can't create it's own money, and it can't borrow money interest free from the Banque De France. Meaning that Brussels is being run by men which have not been elected by the people. And this means that we are being run by a dictatorship."

France Protests Bank-Caused Debt-Slavery Dec 2018, 55 sec
https://www.youtube.com/watch?v=nao0S17iplw

(Brussels is the *de facto* capital of the European Union, as it hosts a number of principal EU institutions)

Please forgive me my analogies, such as comparison between those addicted to money and power, and how their addictions spread pain and addictions to others in society. I see a connection where others may not, and that is just fine.

"Hope has two beautiful daughters; their names are Anger and Courage. Anger at the way things are, and Courage to see that they do not remain as they are."

— St. Augustine of Hippo, (A.D. 354 - 430)

Chapter 16   1976
"Trust for Sale"
U.S. Supreme Court

Money equals speech, right? Wait, **WHAT!!**

This Chapter is about: Trick #9 is about how easy it is to purchase or corrupt government servants in a post-truth world.

It is important because: Humans should know that many highly trusted entities deliver both a "product or service", and also hold a high level of public trust. Some then discover that they can only sell or provide the product or service once, but "trust" can be sold over and over to as many new offers as appear...

"How the Supreme Court and the morbidly rich are ruining democracy in America"

THOM HARTMANN
OCTOBER 30, 2019
People being killed by wildfires in California, and people dying because they can't afford their insulin are the same thing. Both represent the capture of government by corporations — in other words, both are symptoms of democracy in the United States being replaced by a corporate state with little regard for morality, life or the law

In 1976, for the first time in America's history, five conservatives on the U.S. Supreme Court ruled that rich people owning their own personal politicians was constitutionally protected because the money they were using to buy legislators and legislation was "free speech." The case was Buckley v. Valeo. In 1978, SCOTUS extended that logic to corporations in First National Bank of Boston v. Bellotti.

The result was predictable. Rich people and corporations rose up and took over the government, as money poured into Reagan's coffers and the corporate-funded GOP began to dominate the American political scene. And, also predictably, the most predatory and least scrupulous among those billionaires and corporations ended up with the most influence.

This Supreme Court-written law, reaffirmed in 2010's Citizens United decision, was never proposed by any legislature, governor, or president, and, in fact, struck down a series of "good government" laws restricting money in politics that went all the way back to 1907.

And it has largely reduced democracy in the United States to its trappings. The public is engaged in a series of rather empty rituals, at least for the moment.

A representative democracy, of course, is generally agreed to mean that the majority of the people vote for what they want from government and most often then get it via the people they elected. When the majority wanted, for example, the right to unionize, a minimum wage, unemployment insurance, Social Security, civil rights laws, and Medicare, our government brought those things into existence.

All that was, of course, before the Supreme Court eradicated what democracy we had in 1976 and 1978.

Those decisions brought a river of money into politics and thus swept Reagan into office. He did pretty much everything his donors wanted and screwed the rest.

In a 1938 speech to Congress, FDR said:
"The liberty of a democracy is not safe if the people tolerate the growth of private power to a point where it becomes stronger than their democratic state itself. That, in its essence, is fascism — ownership of government by an individual, by a group, or by any other controlling private power."

https://www.salon.com/2019/10/30/how-the-supreme-court-and-the-morbidly-rich-are-ruining-democracy-in-america_partner/?fbclid=IwAR0ZpueDMCkfWNse4MCtK0AhCVLxzt5Gdi95rrgkP5Fz-UQCjg6r3hujveDY

Chapter 17   1999
Glass Steagall Act Repealed

This Chapter is about: Letting banks resume their gambling spree that was believed to have caused the first Depression. Farming Humans trick #10 is when bankers tell governments how to rig public rules…to benefit only bankers.

It is important because: Taxpayers must not only buy the champagne but also suffer the losses for the next (2020?) depression.

"In 1999 Congress passed the Gramm–Leach–Bliley Act, also known as the Financial Services Modernization Act of 1999, to repeal them. Eight days later, President Bill Clinton signed it into law."

What "it" was, was the repeal of the social and economic protections from bank gambling on investments with bank depositor's money. It was called the Glass Steagall Act.

In 1933, in the wake of the 1929 stock market crash and during a nationwide commercial bank failure and the Great Depression, two members of Congress put their names on what is known today as the Glass-Steagall Act. This act separated investment and commercial banking activities. At the time, "improper banking activity," or what was considered overzealous commercial bank involvement in stock market investment, was deemed the main culprit of the financial crash. According to that reasoning, commercial banks took on too much risk with depositors' money. Additional, and sometimes non-related, explanations for the Great Depression evolved over the years, and many questioned whether the GSA hindered the establishment of financial services firms that can equally compete against each other.
BY REEM HEAKAL of Investopedia

"Some argue that the repeal of the Glass-Steagall Act of 1933 caused the financial crisis because banks were no longer prevented from operating as both commercial and investment banks, and repeal allowed banks to become substantially larger, or "too big to fail."

The repeal of the Glass-Steagall Act of 1933, (seen earlier in our timeline) gave bankers a free pass to go back to risking taking with customer bank deposits.

Billions could be made by betting the bank, and if the banks lost, they could count upon the government (read "taxpayers") to bail them out. "We must bail them out, they are too big to fail, the economy depends upon them",…(plus they now own our governments).

This was the assumed cause of the Great Depression of the 1930's, and it was for this reason that the Glass Steagal Act was put into place. It's removal in 1999 granted banks the right to play games with the economic safety of the entire country, knowing they would be rescued if they lost.

It's removal also gives another example of how dangerous it is when public servants discover that they can make a personal fortune by selling out the public trust…to as many offers as come to the table.

That is one of the hallmarks of an unfair or corrupted financial and political system. A system that farms taxpayers and sells the public out, instead of serving them as promised in law.

The 2008 housing and mortgage bubble collapse (and bailout) would follow only nine years following the repeal of Glass-Steagal. Another bubble burst and another round of fresh-printed money went to reward Fed member banks for their various addictions. They (banks) get all their losses back, and the US public pays… forever. This would be pure-genius if it were not such a criminal breach of the public trust.

How much money could you make if your gambling addiction gave you all of your winnings, and your losses were bailed out by taxpayer money from a friendly government? How many yachts would you own? (and how much could you make as a politician with the ability to re-sell your "public trust" to as many good offers as appear?)

Also known as Glass-Steagall, the Banking Act of 1933 effectively separated risky speculative investment banking from traditional, FDIC protected functions like issuing mortgages and small business loans. The repeal of this law by Bill Clinton in 1999 led directly to the toxic mortgage-fueled meltdown of 2008... the root cause of our current economic situation.

Banks are helping themselves to taxpayer-funded money in the trillions. During the Savings and Loan crisis of the 1980's, banks learned that government bailouts will prop them up if they lose, so there is no incentive to be careful, No reason to not "bet the farm", so to speak.

Looting a nation is this easy. Simply rig laws and belief systems so that poverty is not a possibility for 0.1% of the population, and prosperity will become less possible for large portions of society. It is like repealing the financial laws of gravity, but only for a few men.

The Glass Steagall Act was put into place for public protection, and removing these protections left the US taxpayer "holding the bag" for the gambling losses of the richest "persons" on the planet. It provides guaranteed prosperity for banks, lawyers, politicians and the well connected insiders, with lowered levels of poverty for all who are not on the inside.   It is organized systemic corruption by professionals and public servants.

> *"You have the right to fail. You just do not have the right to cause other people to fail."*
> Lou Holtz, Fighting Irish Notre Dame Football coach 1986-1996

Clinton released a statement on the signing of the Gramm-Leach-Bliley Act which said that the legislation would stimulate "greater innovation and competition in the financial services industry." Today, just five Wall Street mega banks control the majority of assets of the more than 5,000 banks and savings associations that exist in the U.S. today. These same Wall Street banks are allowed to charge upwards of 17 percent or more on consumer credit cards while paying 1 percent or less to their depositors. Simply put, Clinton launched a massive wealth transfer system in America.

Clinton said this at the signing ceremony:
"The Gramm-Leach-Bliley Act makes the most important legislative changes to the structure of the U.S. financial system since the 1930s. Financial services firms will be authorized to conduct a wide range of financial activities, allowing them freedom to innovate in the new economy. The Act repeals provisions of the Glass-Steagall Act that, since the Great Depression, have restricted affiliations between banks and securities firms. It also amends the Bank Holding Company Act to remove restrictions on affiliations between banks and insurance companies. It grants banks significant new authority to conduct most newly authorized activities through financial subsidiaries. Removal of barriers to competition will enhance the stability of our financial services system."

Nine years later, the U.S. financial system collapsed along with iconic, century old names on Wall Street as the U.S. entered the worst economic collapse since the Great Depression. This is round II. Pam Martens, Wall Street on Parade. April 21, 2020

Chapter 18   2010
Citizens United
U.S. Supreme Court sells out the U.S. (again)

Money equals speech, right? (Wait a minute…didn't they just do this back on page 91?)

This Chapter is about: "In 2008 the most you could contribute to a political campaign was $2800." Bill Maher

It is important because: "Ten years later the most you could contribute was infinite." Bill Maher, Farming Humans Trick #11.

Citizens United was a January 2010 US Supreme Court ruling that threw out the ban on financing candidates. It gave the green light to spend unlimited amounts of money on ads and other political tools, calling for the election or defeat of individual candidates.

The court's decision said it was okay for corporations and unions to spend as much as they want to convince people to vote for or against a candidate.

This led to the creation of super PACs, which act as shadow political parties. They accept unlimited donations from people, corporations and unions and use it to buy advertising, most of it negative.

Super PACs, officially known as "independent expenditure-only political action committees," may engage in unlimited political spending (on, for example, ads) independently of the campaigns, but are not allowed to either coordinate or make contributions to candidate campaigns or party coffers.

Political action committee - Wikipedia

In 2015, author and talk show host Thom Hartmann asked former President Jimmy Carter about Citizens United and the idea of money as speech.

Thom Hartmann talks with President Jimmy Carter, 39th President of the United States. Here Carter comments on the "Citizens United" decision and the "unlimited bribery" that it introduced into American politics.

Transcript:

PRESIDENT JIMMY CARTER: It violates the essence of what made America a great country in its political system.

Now it is just an oligarchy with unlimited political bribery being the essence of getting the nomination for president or elected president. And the same thing applies to U.S. senators and congress members.

We've seen a complete subversion of our political system as a payoff to major contributors, who want and expect and sometimes get favors for themselves after the election is over.

What can be done to change this?

JIMMY CARTER: It is going to take a horrible disgraceful series of acts that turns the public against it, and maybe even the Congress and Supreme Court, that would be the main thing.

But at the present time, the incumbents, Democrats and Republicans look upon this unlimited money as a great benefit to themselves.

Somebody who already is in Congress has a lot more to sell to an avid contributor than someone who is just a challenger.

Related Topics: Jimmy Carter, Citizens United, Election 2016

This Supreme Court decision, was never proposed by any legislature, governor, or president, and, in fact, struck down a series of "good government" laws restricting money in politics that went all the way back to 1907.

In order to farm humans you must build belief systems and systems of governance which are unfair, unjust, and able to diminish average citizens, by elevating the status, needs and influence of a certain few. A "rigged" system where people are separated into categories of inequality, where a privileged few are given special advantages which are not available to all.

Citizens United v. Federal Election Commission, 558 U.S. 310 (2010), is a landmark United States Supreme Court case concerning campaign finance. The Court held that the free speech clause of the First Amendment prohibits the government from restricting independent expenditures for political communications by corporations, including nonprofit corporations, labor unions, and other associations.

The case arose after Citizens United, a conservative non-profit organization, sought to air and advertise a film critical of Democratic presidential candidate Hillary Clinton shortly before the 2008 Democratic primary elections. This violated the 2002 Bipartisan Campaign Reform Act, which prohibited any corporation or labor union from making an "electioneering communication" within 30 days of a primary or 60 days of an election, or making any expenditure advocating the election or defeat of a candidate at any time.

In a majority opinion joined by four other justices, Associate Justice Anthony Kennedy held that the Bipartisan Campaign Reform Act's prohibition of all independent expenditures by corporations and unions violated the First Amendment's protection of free speech.

The ruling effectively freed labor unions and corporations to spend money on electioneering communications and to directly advocate for the election or defeat of candidates. In his dissenting opinion, Associate Justice John Paul Stevens argued that Court's ruling represented "a rejection of the common sense of the American people, who have recognized a need to prevent corporations from undermining self government."

(Wikipedia)

In America it takes a great deal of "attention getting" to reach out to 300 million-plus people, and gain the attention of those who vote. That takes money in todays world, and the candidates with the most money seem able to influence the most voters.

It stands to reason that by letting money equal speech, when it comes to elections or systems of governance, the voice of American people has been silenced or sold out. It's been rigged so that people who own or control corporations, have gained unfair political advantage over the rest. This another example of where a small number of people are "more equal than others."

There is a clear connection between money and power. Candidates know this and it allows them to be swayed into making promises or decisions, based on a "quid pro quo" that might get them into power.

This bends the arc of governance towards those with the most money, and if the most money in a rigged system often involves illegal, immoral, unjust or unfair acts, then illegal, immoral, unjust or unfair players get to gain influence in the country, or at very least they can "out-influence" the average voter. Farming humans in favor of corporate interests, instead of serving humans, then becomes the name of the game.

It might also tend to benefit candidates who can lie the best, who sell out the public, or who can "shape shift" in order to gain the power, with no intention of actually serving society. Citizens end up being governed by it's weakest members instead of the strongest, and the results show up in nations today.

Many "advanced" countries are no longer the democracies that they claim to be, and instead more closely resemble Oligarchy or Plutocracy:

Oligarchy, "government by the few, especially despotic power exercised by a small and privileged group for corrupt or selfish purposes. Oligarchies in which members of the ruling group are wealthy or exercise their power through their wealth are known as **plutocracies**."
https://www.britannica.com/topic/oligarchy

The video which does a good job of painting this picture in under 8 minutes, for those who need a visual, is worth watching and is titled, "Money Equals Speech" and is found on YouTube.

https://www.youtube.com/watch?v=DWuM4Jyd_sw

In an attempt to create solutions, the following is from November 9th, 2019, by CNN:

Rep. Adam Schiff on Wednesday introduced a constitutional amendment to overturn the Supreme Court's Citizens United decision, which helped usher in a new era of big money in American elections.

"Our democracy is not for sale. We must stop the flood of dark money from drowning out the voices of everyday citizens," the California Democrat said in a statement on Twitter. He said such an amendment would "restore power to the American people."

By a 5-4 ruling, the high court in 2010 swept aside a ban on independent spending by corporations and unions in candidate elections, saying the restrictions amounted to censorship. Outside spending in federal elections has soared from $338 million in 2008, the last presidential election before the ruling, to $1.4 billion in 2016, according to the nonpartisan Center for Responsive Politics.

Overturning the blockbuster ruling has become a rallying cry for many progressives in the Democratic Party, and other lawmakers have introduced a similar measure this year. But efforts to revise the Constitution have failed to gain traction.

https://www.cnn.com/2019/05/08/politics/schiff-constitutional-amendment/index.html?fbclid=IwAR0nF8gxTqmnDT4OMQQkep-P06oBKdvolhAQSLeQJoxagguSRhMpgJH95cz4

Another interesting commentary on how American democracy no longer represents the people, is found in a Ted Talk by Larry Lessig. "Tweedism" is simple corruption, and it is working perfectly in our governance systems.

Larry Lessig demonstrates how only .02% of the population of the nation, get to choose the leadership nominees in **both China and America.** He presents a funny, witty tale of how corruption is built into the design of American democracy.

It is time for modern day people to start telling themselves the bitter truth, instead of swallowing lies. The bitter truth is that modern day politics is often nothing but a theater of the absurd and a performance drama for the lazy, to give the public the easy pill to swallow. Perhaps it always has been mere theatre…

Politicians, and many milkmaids, including the media are running a long con game in many democratic societies.

"Our democracy no longer represents the people. Here's how we fix it" | Larry Lessig | TEDxMidAtlantic

https://www.youtube.com/watch?v=PJy8vTu66tE&t=420s

Dr. Lessig's Ted Talk is twenty minutes of fun, informed video in which he lays out the problem and also provides common sense solutions. If you watch the last two minutes, you get a glimpse of what Rosa Parks was likely motivated by when she refused to give up her seat in an Alabama public transit bus, triggering events which changed civil rights in America. It is a must see.

Lawrence Lessig is the Roy L. Furman Professor of Law and Leadership at Harvard Law School, former director of the Edmond J. Safra Center for Ethics at Harvard University, and founder of Rootstrikers, a network of activists leading the fight against government corruption. He has authored numerous books, including Republic, Lost: How Money Corrupts Our Congress—and a Plan to Stop It, Code and Other Laws of Cyberspace, Free Culture, and Remix.

No consensus exists on how to define democracy, but legal equality, political freedom and rule of law have been identified as important characteristics. These principles are reflected in all eligible citizens being equal before the law and having equal access to legislative processes.
Wikipedia

When I ran across this definition of Democracy I was startled at *"equal before the law"*, and *"having equal access to legislative processes"*, both principles have been removed in so many "democratic" countries. Do we now have a "derivative" of democracy, rather than democracy as it was intended? *(see"What does it mean if something is a derivative?" on page 271)*

It makes me wonder if principles of democracy and equality can be so easily cheated by social constructs and man-made belief systems, ("hey...let's invent an artificial thing called a corporation, and lets pretend the people who own this thing can never be held accountable for its actions..."). Is the rest of society simply supposed to accept their new status as second class citizens? Will they even know or understand what has been stolen away from them? How *would* they know?

Finally, I must comment that while much of my writing in this book has reference to the USA, it does not mean I am singling them out as the worst example. In fact, they appear so much on my radar due to their global influence and importance, and the significant amount of information about them. My own country of Canada on the other hand, is even less transparent, and has less disclosure of the inner workings of governance systems. Our country's choice to stay with the British, rather than toss them out, allows for considerably less openness and transparency.

How Democracies Die is a 2018 book by Harvard University political scientists Steven Levitsky and Daniel Ziblatt about how elected leaders can gradually subvert the democratic process to increase their power.

How Democracies Die - Wikipedia

"The rule of law" is often nothing other than a series of mental narratives which are treated as reality by existing power structures"
Caitlin Johnstone

Chapter 19

A Derivative Revolution?

This Chapter is about: Seeing the many meanings of the word "derivative", not all of which pertain to complex or artificial financial creations. Farming Humans Trick #12 is when a few men have the power to create almost anything they desire...out of nothing.

It is important because: Could we be seeing the effects of "Derived Persons", creating "Derived Money" when "artificial persons" can be now be created using nothing but paper and lawyers? Can we cheat the "all men created equal"?

Reader Reminder!: Keep in mind that this book is part "thought experiment". I put it out there there to bounce the concepts on others, in hopes of better understanding it myself.

=========

The agricultural revolution rose from improved farming techniques and practices that led to massive increases in food production.

The industrial revolution created mechanical systems and machines to serve man, and reduce the dependance on human muscle or harnessed animal power.

The technology revolution created electronic machines which began to serve man, and still do, but entire technology systems seem able to become harnessed and morphed into systems which a few men can entirely control. Such dominance in the hands of a few men can then be used to control and influence millions or billions of people who use that technology. It is the opposite of Nicolas Talib's concept of "antifragile", in that it creates the most fragile structures in history, when just a few men can control giant aspect of society. It makes society fragile, and no longer robust.

> What if a change from "machines serving man", to "man serving machines" has happened using technology? Signs of this have began to appear in the fog of the 21st Century.

The artificial "person" (the Corporation) was created to serve an elite class of men, and today much of humanity now serves this creation, this "machine". Today, in 2020, we have an ever smaller circle of billionaires controlling these ever larger technology systems which we now all rely upon. Data "bits" are the new unregulated game it seems.

Lawyers were a "professional class" of people, derived from the everyday population to serve Kings and other members of the upper classes. Over time many lawyers morphed into specialists who serve the invisible or artificial "persons" that we call corporations. Corporations themselves are something "derived" out of thought experiments and belief systems.

This gives us:

1. A professional class of persons (Lawyers. Belief system #1)

2. Working for artificially created "persons" (Corporations. Belief system #2)

3. To grant them elevated legal benefits (Belief system #3)

4. In a society which no human on earth can obtain those same benefits...(except humans who own artificially created persons, Corporations)

5. If that is horribly complex, and headache inducing, you will see why it works so well...because any sane human would not bother to *even try* to figure out what this leads to.

The "derivative revolution" (if I may call it that...and it *is* my thought experiment after all:) has allowed clever men to capitalize upon traits of human gullibility, to create,

(1) new money systems (to their personal advantage),
(2) new financial products (to their personal advantage),
(3) new legal and corporate belief systems (to their personal advantage).
(4) Political systems which serve Corporations while claiming to serve the public.
(5) These systems act together using new technology (to their further advantage) allow the mass farming of humans on a scale never before imagined.
(6) All these derived creations deliver unique advantages over every other "person" on the planet. It is the equivalent of if lawyers repealed the laws of gravity but ONLY for their clients, and we all believed them and walked around like we had an invisible weight on our backs.

Gullibility is a failure of social intelligence in which persons are easily tricked or manipulated into ill-advised courses of action. It is closely related to credulity, which is the tendency to believe unlikely propositions that are unsupported by evidence.
Wikipedia

Humanity is simply unable to stand on equal footing while a few billionaires control corporate "machines" that combine advanced technology with limited liability, and unlimited ability to do harm without real consequences. Artificially derived "persons", creating artificially derived money, and artificially created rules and belief systems to place one tiny class of humans in charge, and the rest in charge of paying the debt for it all. What a great lawyer-derived game of "lets pretend..."

Recall the principles of democracy being "…all eligible citizens being *equal before the law* and having equal access to legislative processes."
With control of technology and using an artificial person, the excuse can always be:
<u>*I did not do it, my invisible friend did…*</u>

We have created creatures which can get away with draining cheating or robbing entire societies, and the unique twist is that

the creatures doing the robbing often <u>*are*</u> the banks, or some other giant entity, and the robbing without justice or accountability is done upon society.

It is a criminal "win win", and a loss for society. I do not mean that all corporations are abusive to humanity, but the opportunity now exists to easily get away with financial, social, and political murder.

Corporate owners are double-insulated when they can hide behind management, plus their limited-liability for the owners of the corporation. Perhaps triple-insulated above other humans when corporate lawyers step in to protect them. Add a few politicians onto the quid pro quo payroll, and farming humans is no longer the exception, it becomes the Gresham's Law-like norm. (Greshams law: The bad always drives out the good)

Within the above, an invisible, artificially derived "person" was created with limited accountability and near perfect immunity to human systems of justice. Those "persons" have become giants of the kind that 1950's Sci-fi novels were made…unstoppable killer-beasts that can affect millions of humans.

I call this the "Derivative Revolution" to try and put a name to the concept. Like many financial derivatives, building something based on derivatives of reality is like building a house of cards.

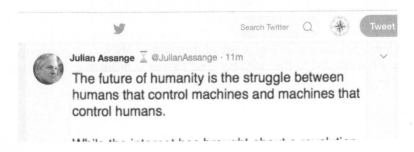

Chapter 20
2020 Derivatives of Truth?

This Chapter is about: Corrupting public information.

It is important because: Dis-information allows humans to be confused, distracted and taken advantage of. Trick #13

"Facebook will continue to allow false claims in political ads"

In the news today (Jan 10, 2020) Mark Zuckerberg's Facebook allows falsified political ads to be put onto the popular social media site.
"The social media company also will not restrict features that let political advertisers target ads to tiny segments of Facebook users, it said in a Thursday blog post."

https://nypost.com/2020/01/09/facebook-will-continue-to-allow-false-claims-in-political-ads/

Facebook has become a profiteer of the Cambridge Analytica style of influence peddling and election rigging. By singling out specific Facebook users who almost never vote, and using targeted false information to influence them into action, they can influence election results. Certainly Facebook will benefit financially from this, but is it "Derivative News" or contribution to a "Derivative of Democracy"?

We saw indicators of this in the 2016 U.S. presidential election, when Cambridge Analytica executives were recorded as using this voter-push strategy to affect political outcomes in many countries. Those who recall seeing unusual things on the news in North America, like young Nazi's marching in the streets of America might recall what this strategy looks like.

When "money equals speech" it allows corporate money to influence voters, and use false claims (lies) to interfere with elections. It causes democracies to be taken over by great wealth and those who peddle derivatives of truth.

I look back to just 20 years ago, when my computer and phone were tools, and I was using them to run a business and make life better. Today, the ability to immerse the public in lies or false-hoods, while farming private data for the benefit of technology, it appears that _I am now the tool_…and technology is _using me_ to gain greater profit, and greater power. This too, is Farming Humans.

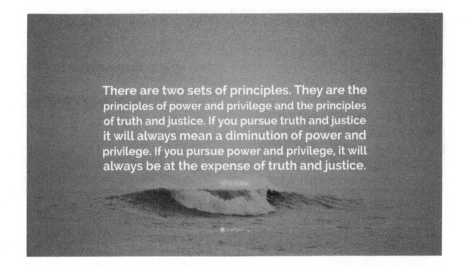

There are two sets of principles. They are the principles of power and privilege and the principles of truth and justice. If you pursue truth and justice it will always mean a diminution of power and privilege. If you pursue power and privilege, it will always be at the expense of truth and justice.

Chapter 21
If The "Advice" Is Free
The Product Is...You

This Chapter is about: Farming investor's financial returns.

It is important because: Most financial "advisors" are not what they seem. Farming Humans Trick #14

> "If you look around the poker table and you can't spot the patsy, you're it." Warren Buffett

The are so many elements of farming humans that I won't pretend to know all, but the first one I found close to home, and it is how I began to see the rest.

I worked in the brokerage industry before banks were majority owners, and also after banks purchased 90% of investment firms. Recall that the repeal of Glass Steagall by Bill Clinton in the 1990's allowed banks back into the investment business.

All that stands in the way of banks and investment dealers farming the public, was the capture of the regulatory bodies, the men and women who "stand up for the public interest". It turns out that for a few tens of millions of dollars (give or take) any regulatory body in the world can be entirely funded, and hundreds of billions can then be quietly harvested by taking advantage of the public, with the help of those financially captured "regulators".

Case in point, it used to be that financial "advice" was something that wealthy people paid for, and they received experience advice in return. (see Securities Acts 1936, 1940 etc)

Stock brokers, and investment salesmen (few women were allowed back then) could only give "advice" on an investment transaction if it were "solely incidental" to the sales transaction.

"Solely incidental" was (and still is) the term found in the US Securities law (Sec 202, INVESTMENT ADVISERS ACT OF 1940) that legislated the responsibilities in the industry.

In loose terms it meant that the broker (salesperson) was not able to give advice, unless it was of such minor proportions as to be "solely incidental to the conduct of his business as a broker..."

For example if the broker wanted Mrs. Jones to sell one of her bank stocks to purchase a new tech stock, the question of *which* bank stock Mrs. Jones should sell is something that might fit into the "solely incidental" category of advice.

This provided separation between investment "advice", and "investment products". If the advice is not paid for, i.e., if it is "Free" such as with the person falsely saying "trust me, I am an advisor", then you, the customer are paying a fee or commission for the investment *product* and not for *advice*. That leaves the non-fiduciary "advisor" *free to sell you out* by secretly serving a third party, namely the dealer who signs their paycheck, or a mutual fund with bigger kickbacks to the disguised sales agent.

> Search the differences between "Fiduciary vs Suitability" for greater understanding.

Sales and advice are two different roles with entirely different qualifications and legal responsibilities to investors. Virtually no investor I have met is allowed to learn of this clever trick and billions are farmed each year from an unsuspecting public which is not informed of the differences. Thanks to helpful "regulators" who are on the money-side of the game.

If that does not make sense, see Warren Buffet's explanation in the biography, "SNOWBALL", by Alice Schroeder. In the book Buffet uses a medical analogy to describe the different roles between "advice provider" and "product seller". He uses the analogy of the medical industry "advice prescriber" (a doctor), or the "pill salesman" (drug sales rep). Buffet worked in both investment salesperson and investment adviser roles during his career and he knows this difference better than anyone on the planet.

The advisor or adviser vowel-movement trick, gives nearly one million financial "pill sellers" in North America a clever, yet deceptive way of influencing how the public invests. It allows 90-day-qualified sales reps, to pretend to be financial "doctors". All it takes is a few thousand well paid regulators. ("say…did he say he was an "adviser, or an advisor?") The public never asks their doctor whether their medical license is spelled "Doctor" or "Docter", and the financial industry has learned to use that "vowel movement" trick to their billion dollar profit advantage.

They simply "imply", without having to deliver, a fiduciary duty of care to the investor. They lead 99.99% of investors (virtually all retail investors) to "assume" that they have the same kind of investment guy as the 0.01% have.

Picture your life savings and investments, in the hands of a former pill seller from Perdue Pharmaceutical, the folks who pushed dangerously addictive opioids upon millions of people, many of whom were pushed…to death. But to a pill seller, this is "sales success", and big sales earns a big bonus.

The investment sales industry, like the drug sales industry is an "eat what you kill" business, where the seller is only paid if sales are made or assets are gathered for fees.

I witnessed the transformation as a young man, when I was told that I was no longer a broker, but an investment "advisor",. I understood that to mean what most of the public assumes…while the less naive sales brokers and managers around me seemed to understand that the game was to be the biggest financial "pill seller" if you wanted to get ahead. Even if some clients got financially murdered in the sales-race.

It was (and is today in 2020) a fraudulent misrepresentation, but that does not seem important. The important item is…"is it profitable?" Perhaps even more importantly, "can we get away with it?" Yes, if we fund nearly all financial regulators in North America. Class actions and breach of trust criminal actions come to mind for investors who have been duped by a simple vowel movement…and thousands of deeply conflicted regulators.

How much money could you take from the public, if you were able to take a 90 day training course, and then represent yourself as a Doctor, Dentist, Lawyer, Engineer or Financial Advisor? What if you were only a commission selling agent? Would that be fraud? That is what hundreds of thousands of investment sales agents have accomplished due to the magic of "self" regulation.

Faking most professional titles will land you in jail for fraud, while the advisor title could land you in a new condo…if you can gather enough assets and sell the "right" products.

In case it might help illustrate the risks to your retirement security:

As I was working on this portion of the book, my father-in-law was going through heart and lung troubles at age 84. The respiratory therapist who provided him with Oxygen in his home was so helpful and professional, that I gave him some info as a thank you. I told him that my passion was in making sure that people who work, save and invest to retire, get as much of the rightful benefit of that effort as possible. I said that the difference between a registered investment professional, and a fake one, is enough to cut the retirement "oxygen" that he must retire and live on, from a level of about 95 percent, to a level of half of that, or less.

The story fit for a couple of reasons. One being that we had just spent an informative half hour with him, learning about how to raise grandpa's blood oxygen level from the 80 percent range, into the 90 percent range. The second being that the average "skim", or financial harm, inflicted upon the average investor, by false "advisors", is in the range of 2% to 3% each year in Canada.

A skim of 2% to 3% of your investment returns each year, when compounded over 30 or 35 years is sufficient to cut your future life savings by more than half. That is like investing for 35 years with the help of a falsified "professional", thinking you will retire with everything you deserve, and discovering when it is too late, that you are missing half or even two-thirds of what you should own. This is how to really farm humans.

I thanked him for his expertise and for this analogy, that the skimming of investment returns by a false "advisor" is a bit analogous to a falsified or faked respiratory therapist who could somehow siphon away a few percent of your Oxygen, over a lifetime, and when you need it the very most, you will be living on 33% of what you truly needed to survive, when you were led to believe you would have 93%. It is only a thought experiment, but one that hopes to illustrate the damage to society done when investors do not know the difference between a self titled "advisor" and a professional fiduciary "adviser".

I hope that explanation is not too distracting for readers at this stage, and I thank you for letting me squeeze it in.

Speaking of Haircuts…

Each time I get a haircut, I ask the person doing the work how much training they needed to get their license to cut hair.

Whether it is 2000 hours of training in Nevada, or 2500 hours in Utah, or somewhere in between in Canada it never fails to amaze me to see the one to two year requirements needed to train, and then apprentice, before being able to cut my hair.

When chatting with them, I ask them if they know they could be calling themselves an investment "advisor" and "handling" peoples life savings with as little as a 90 day training. They are always shocked to hear that.

I understand their shock. After all, one is given the impression that a financial advisor is a highly trained and skilled financial professional who requires years, if not decades of experience and training to do the job.

Here is the kicker….to become a financial "Advis_er_" (see "fiducia-ry") it *does* require years to get there.

However to falsely call yourself a financial "advis_or_", (bank, investment and insurance product sellers) requires only 90 days in many jurisdictions. (even less if you purchase an "exemption" from registration requirements from the securities commission)

See "Investment Advisor Bait and Switch, GET YOUR MONEY BACK!" on YouTube   https://www.youtube.com/watch?v=KH6XMXlfdBw&t=23s

Fiduciaries must:
- Put their clients' best interests before their own, seeking the best prices and terms.
- Act in good faith and provide all relevant facts to clients.
- Avoid conflicts of interest and disclose any potential conflicts of interest to clients.
- Do their best to ensure the advice they provide is accurate and thorough.
- Avoid using a client's assets to benefit themselves, such as by purchasing securities for their own account before buying them for a client.

Fiduciary duty is a legal responsibility to put the interests of another party before your own. If someone has a fiduciary duty to you, he or she must act solely in your financial interests.

A fiduciary cannot, for example, recommend a strategy that doesn't benefit you, or provides them a kickback. You can think of it like the doctor-patient relationship, where one party has a duty to put the other party's interests first.

Fiduciary duty is important for guiding the actions of professionals who deal with clients' money. It's also important because, when violated, it provides an avenue to legal action.
A breach of fiduciary duty occurs when a fiduciary fails to honor his or her obligation.

Sources for further reading:

- Securities Act of 1933
- Securities Exchange Act of 1934
- Investment Company Act of 1940
- Investment Advisers Act of 1940
- Sarbanes-Oxley Act of 2002
- Dodd-Frank Wall Street Reform and Consumer Protection Act of 2010

Objective financial information is found at credible sources such as The Consumer Federation of America, and others like them. Try to avoid seeking financial advice from those who sell financial products. That is like asking a barber if you need a haircut...

=========

Hidden in the fine print of the regulator (FINRA) which oversee's "brokers", in the U.S. is the following clue to the long con.

Investment Advisers

"Although most people would use an "o," we purposely spell adviser with an "e" when we talk about investment advisers. That's because the laws that govern this type of investment professional spell the title this way."

"Many investment advisers are also brokers—but these two types of investment professional aren't the same. So as you choose among different professionals, here's what you need to know about investment advisers."

"What they are: An investment adviser is an individual or company who is paid for providing advice about securities to their clients. Although the terms sound similar, investment advisers are not the same as financial advisors and should not be confused. The term financial advisor is a generic term that usually refers to a broker (or, to use the technical term, a registered representative). By contrast, the term investment adviser is a legal term that refers to an individual or company that is registered as such with either the Securities and Ex-

change Commission or a state securities regulator. Common names for investment advisers include asset managers, investment counselors, investment managers, portfolio managers, and wealth managers. Investment adviser representatives are individuals who work for and give advice on behalf of registered investment advisers."

https://www.finra.org/investors/learn-to-invest/choosing-investment-professional/investment-advisers

Investor solutions could come through class actions, which may exceed the size of tobacco or chemical industry cases. That, and/or criminal actions against regulators and others who have intentionally breached the public trust while claiming to act in a public protective capacity. RICO (Racketeering) comes to mind.

Placing ones trust and life savings into the hands of a commission sales agent, while under the impression that the agent is a fiduciary investment professional, is responsible for millions of investors having to work an extra ten or twenty years, or retiring with half as much money as they could have had if only they knew of the truth.

It is another example of using a fraud, and thousands of paid-regulators to farm the public under a false disguise of protecting the public.

"Self regulation to a "suitability" standard will find almost anything suitable...especially if it pays a lot of commission."
Kathy Waite

Chapter 22

Corporations Now Wear The Ring of Gyges,
The Power To Commit Crime And Say, "I Did Not Do It, My Invisible Friend Did"

This Chapter is about: A new class of "person" was created in 1886. Further to Farming Humans Trick #6, this is how "all men are created equal", got quietly violated.

It is important because: Millions of people are no longer "equal"... thanks to a few lawyers.

Today in 2020, corporations, public and privately owned, have become some of the largest creatures on the planet, and yet they get all the rights of persons. They exist but only on paper and only through belief systems which give them their special attributes.

Looking back, some of these attributes may not have been done with regard for fairness to the public. Some are nothing more than social and legal constructs, and an unintended consequence of their creation is that in some we have allowed the creation of monsters.

Today, corporate "persons" have achieved strength and power far beyond all but a few humans, and power beyond police, prosecutors and governments. The are too big to jail, and impossible to even stop, much less to arrest. If you have not noticed, government prosecutors are also reluctant to prosecute the strongest entities on earth, as it can be a "career limiting" move.

Many governments and public servants now work as servants to corporations, instead of as servants to the public. The money and the power of an untouchable entity gives some corporations the mythical power of the fire breathing dragons found in legends.
 The smart and the clever seek to be on the "inside" of that tribe, while the rest are left wondering why life is so much more difficult

for them. To me I see an image of the killer robots imagined by 1950's Science-fiction creators. Unstoppable giants able to wreak havoc upon society while humans scatter away, powerless to intervene.

Only such a monster would work to destroy as much of the planet as possible, in a race to convert the world's wealth into bits of paper (money) which feeds the corporation, then goes on to feed the masters who own the machines.

More than 2000 years have passed since Plato wrote his "thought experiment" about the Ring of Gyges, the magical ring which would allow man to commit any crime without fear of punishment...and today we have corporations who own that Ring of Gyges...and who do dirty work for the men who own them.

Attributes of Some Corporations
Invincible
Anonymous (shell corps, multiple-layered ownership, offshore corps and numbered corps)
Untouchable
Limited liability
Not-arrestable
Not-jailable
Cannot be criminally charged

Giving every *non-living* (corporate) person added powers of partial invisibility to justice, immunity to arrest and incarceration, limited risk of prosecution, limited liability, and possibly anonymity…while every *real-living* person has no such powers, repeals the fairness, the natural order of things, which I call the principles or laws of poverty and prosperity for the men behind those giant machines. "I did not do it, my invisible friend did", is their get out of jail card.

It allows creation of a powerful Genie-like entity and we call these entities Corporations. This is Farming Humans.

The Delaware Division of Corporations' 2018

This annual report explains why Delaware remains the "Corporation Capital of the World." Always ahead of the trends, with laws that define the industry's cutting edge, Delaware is the state where accountants, attorneys and business professionals from all around the world incorporate.

- 67.2% of the Fortune 500 companies are incorporated in Delaware

- As of the end of 2018, almost 1.4 million entities were incorporated in Delaware.
https://www.delawareinc.com/blog/delaware-adds-over-200k-new-companies-2018/

Chapter 23

REGULATORS AS WOLVES IN DISGUISE?

This Chapter is about: Facade regulators who help industries to harm the public. Farming Humans Trick #15

It is important because: When privately-hired rental-cops pretend to be the law, the public gets abused.

With governments of many nations assuming a submissive servant-like role to large corporations, it did not take long before corporations offered a "helpful" idea to governments.

The helpful idea was in the creation of thousands of regulatory and self-regulatory agencies, each disguised in a manner that suggested a duty of protection for the public. The true interest of the modern-day regulator seems to be to personally glean as much money as possible for oneself, and to follow the instructions and grant the wishes of industry. (which funds them) A search for the term "regulatory capture" turned up the following two descriptions:

Regulatory capture is a corruption of authority that occurs when a political entity, policymaker, or regulatory agency is co-opted to serve the commercial, ideological, or political interests of a minor constituency, such as a particular geographic area, industry, profession, or ideological group. **Wikipedia**

Regulatory capture is an economic theory that says **regulatory** agencies may come to be dominated by the industries or interests they are charged with regulating. The result is that an agency, charged with acting in the public interest, instead acts in ways that benefit the industry it is supposed to be regulating.
Regulatory Capture Definition - Investopedia

I cannot recall the last so-called regulatory body, government or private, that I found *not* captured, influenced or corrupted by it's underlying corporate interests. The public should be aware that what is presented to them as sound public protection is most often little more than an artifice, a facade of regulation, which hides what is truly "industry protection". It is usually so well hidden as to be a perfect crime upon the public.

Whether in resources, energy, finance, pharmaceutical, chemical, aviation, accounting, legal, or a thousand others, regulators and self-regulators today are often a well paid army, a "fifth column" to protect the industry involved, and not the public. Follow the money in any case and you might discover similar. FDA, FAA, SEC, FINRA, OSC, FCA, FCAC, no matter who you search in any developed country you will find millionaire regulator salaries and other incentives to serve the industry that feeds them, while keeping the quid pro quo's hidden.

Hiring and paying ones own regulators is as easy as hiring a private rent-a-cop. In Canada, for about $100 million, the financial industry can fund any of our Securities Commissions, and the ability to then obtain exemptions to the law from the regulator, is by itself worth hundreds of billions. Just ONE exemption to the law, can earn billions. Capturing and funding regulators is the simply best (but corrupt) investment any industry can make.

Another example comes to us from Boeing in late 2019, with the 737 Max, and the news that Boeing's influence over the Federal Aviation Administration (FAA) was powerful enough to allow Boeing *itself to legally approve* its own aircraft, which is like being able to mark your own exams…(or print your own money).

> "…it's much easier to purchase and lead legislators, as we learned this week happened when it was revealed that last year a paid-off member of Congress slipped language into law written by or for Boeing that essentially put them in charge of FAA airworthiness certification. The result was the 737 Max and 346 dead human beings."
> Thom Hartmann

For those who missed the story it went something like this…

A New York Times investigation into the Boeing 737 Max crisis involving two crashes that killed a cumulative 346 people and the continued grounding of the entire line from global service—has found troubling signs that the Federal Aviation Administration process to guarantee the planes' safety was fatally flawed and bent to Boeing pressure when it came to potential hazards.

The Times wrote that after "intense lobbying to Congress by industry" resulted in the *FAA delegating more authority to manufacturers in 2005, an approach that FAA officials believed would streamline approvals, some staff became concerned that they were no longer able to track what was happening inside Boeing.* According to the Times, interviews with over a dozen current and former FAA and Boeing employees have shown that regulators "never independently assessed the risks of the dangerous software known as MCAS [Maneuvering Characteristics Augmentation System] when they approved the plane in 2017."

Additionally, *a two-decade veteran of the FAA who was a leading advocate of delegating authority to manufacturers, Ali Bahrami, left the agency in 2013 to take a lobbying role at the Aerospace Industries Association trade group* where he urged "maximum use of delegation" to Congress. He returned to the FAA in 2017 as the head of safety, the Times noted.

https://www.nytimes.com/2019/07/27/business/boeing-737-max-faa.html

The plight of Boeing shows the perils of modern capitalism. The corporation is a wounded giant. Much of its productive capacity has been mothballed following two crashes in six months of the 737 Max, the firm's flagship product: the result of safety problems Boeing hid from regulators.

"Something is wrong with today's version of capitalism. It's not just that it's unfair. It's that it's no longer capable of delivering products that work. The root cause is the generation of high and persistent profits, to the exclusion of production. We have let financiers take over our corporations. They monopolize industries and then loot the corporations they run."

https://www.theguardian.com/commentisfree/2019/sep/11/boeing-capitalism-deregulation

---

"The corporation is now a political machine with a side business making aerospace and defense products."

Boeing used its political connections to monopolize the American aerospace industry and corrupt its regulators.

"…no one could do anything about it. Customers and suppliers no longer had any alternative to Boeing, and Boeing corrupted officials in both parties who were supposed to regulate it."

High profits result in sloth and corruption. Many of our industrial Goliaths are now run in ways that are fundamentally destructive. General Electric, for instance, was once a jewel of American productive capacity, a corporation created out of George Westinghouse and Thomas Edison's patents for electric systems. Edison helped invent the lightbulb itself, brightening the world.

Today, as a result of decisions made by Jack Welch in the 1990s to juice profit returns, GE slaps its label on lightbulbs made in China. Even worse, if investigator Harry Markopoulos is right, General Electric may in fact be riddled with accounting fraud, a once great productive institution strip-mined by financiers.

https://www.theguardian.com/commentisfree/2019/sep/11/boeing-capitalism-deregulation

Regulators, continued…

Jay Clayton (one SEC Chairman) was a Trump appointee.

As a lawyer he has represented Goldman Sachs, Barkleys, UBS and DeutscheBank. DeutscheBank was reportedly a financier of some of Trump's deals.

He helped Goldman Sachs get a $10 Billion taxpayer bailout from the US Treasury. At his confirmation hearing of March 23, 2017 he was unable to answer even some of the simplest of questions about the proven shady deals put upon the public by Goldman Sachs that helped lead to the greatest economic shock the world had seen in decades. When pressed directly, the best he could offer was "I think those are good questions", without even answering what was asked. https://www.huffingtonpost.ca/entry/who-is-sec-chair-nominee-jay-clayton_n_5b55d2abe4b004fe162fa12c?ri18n=true

Securities Regulation is now infamous for being a securities industry fifth column, whereby industry players take turns rotating into positions of regulatory authority, to ensure that the interests of the financial industry are not interfered with, and the interests of the public are not enforced seriously.

The industry pays regulators hundreds of millions to ensure protection for the money mechanisms that produces hundreds of billions for the industry. The SEC is the only government regulator I have found which is not paid directly by the financial industry, however the SEC's ability to be influenced and captured appears to be fully on par with regulators who are fully funded by the industry itself.

Read **No One Would Listen**: A True Financial Thriller, by Harry Markopolos, about the blind-mice inner workings of the SEC. RICO (Racketeering) statutes could be considered against the organized failure to protect Americans by this agency. In some future accountability scenario it may even happen.

To say that regulatory capture is not happening is to deny the self evident. It would be like saying that the brightest and most ambitious minds in the world, when it comes to the protection of their own money and turf, do not have triple levels of redundancy built into the machine. These minds simply do not operate without having their ducks in a row, far beyond what an ordinary person may comprehend. I know this from decades of observations behind those curtains.

These people have better systems of redundancy, and backup, after backup, after backup, in case of failure, than NASA has on a space mission. No disrespect to NASA (the rocket jockeys), but NASAA (the securities jockeys) began building systems to insulate and protect the financial industry over 100 years ago.

The North American Securities Administrators Association, founded in Kansas in 1919, is the oldest international investor protection organization. NASAA is an association of state securities administrators who are charged with the responsibility to protect consumers who purchase securities or investment advice. Wikipedia

The rewards and returns (quid pro quo's) for those who leave multi million dollar salaries, to take a turn at the helm of a regulatory ship like the SEC, while pretending to protect the public, is sufficient for them to make the move. The public is unaware that regulator's are often serve as wolves in sheep's clothing, and that serves the industry perfectly, for harvesting humans.

Attorney Generals who act as Eric Holder did to let off those responsible for the 2008 financial collapse are yet another example of that triple redundancy.

If a person adds up SEC obfuscation towards the American public, its disregard for the public interest, and its revolving door of persons who move from serving the industry, to the SEC and then back to serving industry, it becomes clear that the SEC is a financial industry "Fifth Column", intended to help the financial industry farm the American public, while abusing the legislative power granted to it by the American Public.

A **fifth column** is any group of people who undermine a larger group from within, usually in favor of an enemy group or nation. The activities of a fifth column can be overt or clandestine. The term originated in terms of military strategies, when it was found quite advantageous in battles to have ones own people secretly working inside and alongside ones enemy.

From the transcript of a 30 second video on Youtube titled, "Sen Ackerman correctly sees SEC Chairman as the enemy of the American people, in 2009."

"...our economy is in crisis Mr. Vollmer we thought the enemy was Mr. Madoff , I think it's you. You were the shield, you were the protector, and you come here and fumble through make-believe answers...Mr. chairman I'm through."

https://www.youtube.com/watch?v=T1kCpgdsCLQ

"This is a stickup, gimme all your money or the Global economy dies..."

This was the effect of the 2008 and later financial bailouts, which were provided by the taxpayer and given to the biggest banks to cover gambling addiction losses.

Their gambling losses were not only bailed out by the American taxpayer, but the US Treasury had to borrow in order for the Fed to print the money issued, to bail out the private banks...who own the Fed. Did I get that right? Because it sounds insane.

The banks who own the Fed actually get paid to issue new money, get free money creation for themselves by virtue of "fractional reserve banking", get to gamble their free money to make billions, and if their bets lose, get the taxpayer to bail them out using more free money.

=========

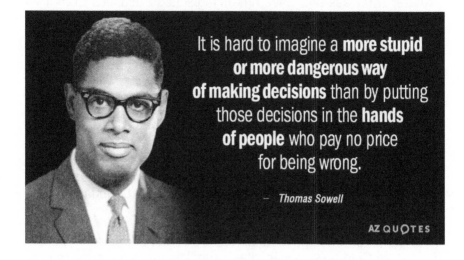

It is hard to imagine a **more stupid or more dangerous way of making decisions** than by putting those decisions in the **hands of people** who pay no price for being wrong.

— *Thomas Sowell*

AZ QUOTES

If you can imagine putting decisions in the hands of people who ***personally profit for doing the wrong thing,*** then you will understand the role of many regulatory bodies today.

What would you say if I told you that a company could gain permission from regulators to conceal or not include certain financial or other statements in securities filings or notices to the public?

They are called exemptions to the law, or "exemptive relief" to securities law in Canada, and are used by the thousands without ever telling the public when and why a company is given permission to skirt the law. It is like knowing that the company wishes to violate the law, and rather than risk getting caught and having to purchase a "deferred prosecution agreement" to hush the crime, they can simply send in a check and an application for "exemptive relief" to whichever financial law they desire to break.

Readers may ask how government legislated Securities Commissions can justify granting secret exemptions to private parties....and what public interest can this serve? They would be correct in asking, and Securities Commissions never say. The only thing they will say is this bit of boilerplate on each exemption approval:

"The principal regulator is satisfied that the decision meets the test set out in the Legislation for the principal regulator to make the decision."

Just a few years back it said, *"The decision maker is satisfied that the decision meets the test set out in the Legislation for the decision maker to make the decision".*

"Decisions" or "exemptive relief" can be searched on Canadian Securities Commission web sites...(until the sites are redacted or removed). Recall that corruption is defined as the use of public power or assets to enrich private parties...

Not only could a Company like VRX (Valeant Pharmaceutical at the time) apply for and receive permission to not need to provide the public with financial statements on the companies that they were acquiring, but it also allowed Trans Mountain Pipeline to conceal a long list of important documents in any prospectus they might create. This helped enrich the owners, when the company was sold to the Canadian government for billions.

I don't know how many extra billions Canadians have lost by the hiding of information like this, but I do know that the market value decline of Valeant Pharmaceutical was in the neighborhood of 80 Billion dollars in lost value. That is a pretty good harvest of the public, for the cost of a simple exemption application at the government securities commission.

80 Billion dollars would be the financial equivalent of about 16 million average property crimes. That is pretty decent money for ONE trick. There are hundreds of exemptions granted in secrecy to insiders each year...to companies who pick and pay our securities "regulators".

Farming the public runs smoothly when financial regulators act as a wholly owned subsidiary of the financial industry that pays them.

Breach of Trust (or RICO) comes to mind when public-legislated bodies can so easily be purchased or morphed into acting contrary to the public interest.

Breach of trust by public officer

Canadian Criminal Code
Every official who, in connection with the duties of their office, commits fraud or a breach of trust, whether or not the fraud or breach of trust would be an offence if it were committed in relation to a private person, is guilty of Canadian Criminal Code Section 122

Passed in 1970, the Racketeer Influenced and Corrupt Organizations Act (RICO) is a US Federal law designed to combat organized crime in the United States. It allows prosecution and civil penalties for racketeering activity performed as part of an ongoing criminal enterprise.

Chapter 23
INDUSTRY "SELF" REGULATORS
Paid To Gaslight The Public

This Chapter is about: Beneath government regulators are layers of industry "self regulators". Trick #17 is to hire your own army of people paid to "gaslight" the public into thinking they are protected.

It is important because: These "self regulatory" layers provides further insulation to shield industry from laws or accountability. The public should be aware of these facades of protection, as they are an essential ingredient in farming humans.

The topic of "Self-regulators" is not a repeat of the previous chapter on government regulators. It is a deeper look into the layers of redundancy and protection for those who farm the public.

Self regulators are a further category of regulators who "self-police" industry behaviors. This category should more accurately be referred to as simple lobby groups, perhaps even cabals.

FINRA is the name of the self regulator for brokers in the U.S.

Sadly, FINRA prevents millions of American investors from being protected from the Adviser/Advisor bait and switch, since FINRA is a regulator of "brokers" only. Brokers are those industry sales agents who have "borrowed" the non-registered title of "Advisor", for its members. The sleight of hand that FINRA performs, is in convincing Americans to trust commission investment sales brokers with their life savings.

The effects of this "borrowed", non-Securities Act title, is to allow millions of Americans life savings to be "advised" by persons who do not hold an SEC or State "Adviser" registration (as the term Advisor implies).

Imagine how much money you could make, if you could take a three-month online sales training program, and then, using a simple ruse, misdirection or "vowel movement", fool the investing public into believing that you were a SEC or State registered fiduciary adviser.

One recent FINRA annual report I checked showed a cash balance of over one billion dollars held by FINRA. I cannot imagine how any regulatory body could accumulate this much money, and it begs the question of how FINRA obtained such riches. Referees are usually not wealthy, unless the are running a "side- game" beneath the public game. The top five execs were sharing about $6 mil in compensation, and cash on hand was over 1/3 Billion (pgs 22 & 26 of 2019 report https://www.finra.org/sites/default/files/2020-06/2019-annual-financial-report.pdf)

If you read the FINRA provided principles below, while they sound good, the information about the false "advisor" bait and switch, is omitted (or concealed) entirely in FINRA public disclosure:

"Every investor in America relies on one thing: fair financial markets. To protect investors and ensure the market's integrity, FINRA is a government-authorized not-for-profit organization that oversees U.S. broker-dealers. We work every day to ensure that everyone can participate in the market with confidence."
- *every investor receives the **basic protections** they deserve;*
- *anyone who sells a securities product has been **tested, qualified and licensed**;*
- *every securities product advertisement used is **truthful**, and not misleading;*
- *any securities product sold to an investor is **suitable** for that investor's needs; and*
- *investors receive **complete disclosure** about the investment product before purchase.*

https://www.finra.org/about

What is missing and hidden in the above statement of principles is worth billions annually and trillions of dollars cumulatively, in my estimation. The false "advisor" bait and switch is cleverly omitted in every line of this information…and what is omitted is billions more valuable that what is included.

Why would governments allow such financial trickery to prey upon vulnerable and financially less-literate people?

Governments are often willing to take the easy route, and "let the industry handle it". It saves them a great deal of money in their budgets, and allows them to avoid responsibility and accountability for the mess. It "insulates" the Senator, Congressman, Minister or other political servant from having to be accountable for complaints of financial abuse of the public. They can simply defer all problems…to the very source of the problem itself. Round and round the victims will go, and the politician is safely out of the picture. It is like putting a drowning victim into the river backwash behind a weir…to make a public drowning problem disappear.

Corporations are allowed to step in and foot the bill, by paying a few hundred millions, to fund *its own regulators*, and also to pay heavily to influence the government regulators like State regulators, the SEC, and Provincial regulators in Canada.

All Thirteen Provincial Securities Commissions in Canada are industry funded. Last I looked there were another 100 or more financial self-regulatory bodies who are also industry funded. Victims of financial industry abuses today face industry obstacles the size of the Rocky Mountains, set up to protect the industry, while mis-labeled as being protective of the public.

Each victim finds themselves alone and in the dark, and each victim has no idea that the regulatory bodies who pretend to "help", are actually throwing them into the backwash just behind the weir. Kangaroo courts is another descriptive term that applies.

Forgive me for beating the "adviser" verses "advisor", and "fiduciary" verses "suitability" argument to death, it was the discovery of this in my own profession that sparked my interest in understanding of how humans farm humans. It is also, in my experience, responsible for draining investors in my country by more money than every other measured crime in the land.

If you will allow me one more analogy:

Suppose you engage someone to "advise" you on your investments, believing that the person you engaged was _duty bound to act only on **your** behalf and acting as **your** agent to advise you._

Now imagine that in secrecy, the person you trust is acting as a _commission sales agent for the investment dealer_, and not acting as an agent on your behalf as you are led to believe. There is a deception of "dual agency" involved in this, or one of "undisclosed dual agency." But "self" regulation ensures that this type of fraud is "unseen".

This is how millions of investors in North America are duped into believing falsified professional credentials, and into investing their life savings under false pretenses.

Imagine how much money the investment selling industry can make by this deceptive bait and switch, with virtually no member of the investing public told of it.

Most regulators and "self"-regulators could be considered the paid, professional "gaslighters" of today. Gaslighting is the deepest kind of moral wrong. When it is practiced by industry regulators to protect their industry, it harms and farms society.

"Imagine you're going through the worst experience you've ever had, and, at the same time, you're being told it's not happening."

Kate Abramson, philosophy professor at the University of Indiana

https://www.theguardian.com/lifeandstyle/2019/mar/02/abuse-prevention-how-to-turn-off-the-gaslighters?fbclid=IwAR1jWv03LH-bzw2LsHZ3QgzM9ZUj7hkqzJlUlcRzyBi7LljzDmAGLTGUAo64

Chapter 25
Markets Breaking Bad
Financial addiction compared to meth addicts.

This Chapter is about: Bankers are free to loot the US Treasury, manipulate markets and enrich themselves at the same time. Farming Humans Trick #17.

It is important because: Systemic looting of taxpayers is done by a very small number of money-addicts who seem willing to do anything to get their fix.

I was in Los Angeles a number of years ago with my son, and we rented a car to explore. When we ran across the downtown area around the Staples Center, we were thrilled. Further exploration led us to the garment district where we ran across the largest population of homeless persons in one place that I had ever witnessed. Remember that I come from a small city in Canada and at that time I had never witnessed people sleeping in cardboard boxes, or under taps or camping tents on city sidewalks. This trip would have been around 2006.

It was like we had stumbled onto a movie-set, or a war zone in downtown Los Angeles. Today I am told the there are over 500,000 homeless in the United States. I am also told that the suicide rate of veterans in the US is now past 58,000, which is roughly how many US soldiers died in the Vietnam war. As my son and I slowly drove the streets of Los Angeles, with our mouths open in astonishment, I did not know what to think. It took years of processing what we saw, to understand even a fraction of its meaning.

What I know now is that we have forced some of society into a Mad Max world where the only remaining rules are the rules of the jungle. That is to say there are no rules....or wait, there are rules for some people, those on the streets live under enforced laws and rules, while those at the top get the gift of living in a no-rules world. Anything goes so long as it makes sufficient money for yourself and for those in your circle, your tribe, or your industry. It reminds me of a 1990's era Dave Chapelle comedy sketch about the different treatment between street criminals and criminals in "suites". Very eye opening to see that it is reality today.

Since that trip to LA, we now see pandemics of homeless, hopeless and addicted people all over the world. It is even here in my own community in Canada, which is something I could not have predicted. I only know that the homeless, helpless and impoverished people in places like LA, and my home town are not the problem. Yes, they **are** a problem...but they are not **the** problem. They are a result of the problem. I know this for certain because I was part of the financial industry that can harm the public with zero repercussions. I saw and learned from the inside what it was like to work in areas where there were virtually no rules applied for abusing humans when it made rich people richer. Imagine a no-rules world. Just hire enough "regulators" and pay them well enough.

It has been an amazing journey to go from an insider, to whistle-blower, to a person able to tell a story, and to understand today's crisis from a unique perspective. Does it make me right? No, but it gives me a different perspective from which to write about what is happening and more importantly why it is happening, and who caused our fall.

Are financial markets today (written pre-covid-2020) an accurate measure of buyers, sellers and economic activity, or are they artificially jacked-up like addicts on Crystal Meth? Are the financial conditions that allow jacked up markets, fueled by drug-like stimulants precisely why millions of people are left behind, left out of the stimulus? The irony of being witness (a clueless witness) to a free money stimulus party since about 1971, which created bubble after bubble after bubble in stocks, yachts, jets, real estate and so on, while 99% of the world had no idea what was happening to them.

Financial markets, fueled by "asset purchases" from the Federal Reserve, have skyrocketed since the 2008 financial bubble and crash. I still believe the Frankenstein experiments in money printing began around the 1970's.

The irony of being able to financially connect the 500,000 home-less persons in the US, and thousands of veteran suicides, with the cost of fighting the Vietnam war fifty years ago, and the loss of 58,000 soldiers in that failed effort...that is rather mind boggling to be able to draw a line, a connection if you will, between todays crisis and yesterdays financial party. A banker's free-money, free-for-all, where the bigger the war, the bigger the payoff...for bankers, insiders, and those with connections. I only hope that enough people get to read this and to make their own conclusions for themselves. Today we are living in the most interesting times, and trying to figure it out is the most interesting thing I can imag-ine.

Homeless people are <u>not</u> the problem...they are the <u>result</u> of the problem. Lets talk about the problem for a change. Lets stop pro-tecting the world's greatest abusers, and letting them hide their Trillion-dollar abuses of society.

========

Bankers are looting the US Treasury to manipulate markets and enrich themselves at the same time. They have gotten away with this for 100 years.

US Citizens are stuck with the tax bill, the broken systems and increased social poverty. I hope that we learn more about financial markets and meth addicts, since they are so similar. The party for those addicted to markets has been the "make it rain" free-money printing game run since 1971. They may call it "Quantitavive Easing", (QE) or "monetary policy" or "Asset purchases by the Fed", or any number of terms which cause 99% of humans to stop listening. I urge everyone to demand better from governments, professionals and public servants. To demand real "service" from those who claim to be in this role. Right now we are letting those addicted to money, play with "self" accountability, which is creating addicts and poverty at a faster rate than our western economies can create prosperity.

"Asset purchases" means the Fed printing money, to give this money to banks in exchange for some of the banks bad assets that need to be purged. How wealthy would your family be if each losing investment could simply be taken off your hands…using borrowed money that the taxpayer must then repay? How poor would your neighbors be if they did not have this money pipeline working for them?

The newly printed money for asset purchases, is backed by US Treasury IOU's, or similar notes and borrowings, for which the public must now repay through income taxes…forever.

Banks thus get billions in freshly created cash, while the US public gets the bad assets, or gets stuck with the bill to pay back the money created to purchase the bad assets. I could probably re-fine that description a bit, but for now I am going to let it lay here. Any corrections are welcomed with gratitude.

Dousing the flames of the 2008 mortgage bubble disaster, using government money issued in this manner, was said to be needed to prevent complete financial system meltdown.

A better choice would have been to let those with a gambling addiction, suffer the consequences of their addiction, like we demand of every addict in Downtown LA. But the Fed is the perfect tool for dumping bank gambling losses and bad assets upon the taxpayer, and to make taxpayers pay to give the banks a clean-money start each time.

The only thing left to do for the recipients of some of those newly printed billions, is to "launder it", to get it out of cash as fast as they can, and into assets that are tangible or real, like any criminal money launderer would do.

After all, the recipients of billions of dollars in money created out of thin air, know better than anyone on the planet, that those bits of colored paper are worthless compared to the assets, the wealth, and the resources, that the colored paper can acquire.

"GET RID OF THE PAPER" are shouts heard in backrooms, and "convert it to something real". Throughout history, bankers and stock jobbers have perfected the art of offering paper promises to humanity, in return for true wealth, blood, sweat and tears.

This might explain the flow of money into real estate, jets, yachts, and stock markets since 2008. Today, in 2020, I cannot see the future, but my instincts tell me that we are going to experience a replay of the first Great American Depression of the 1930's, and that it will happen before the 100 year anniversary of that last one. (Keep in mind the uselessness of such personal premonitions)

(Update September 2020 in light of record setting stock market valuations (for some companies) while economies were still under water) The above made so little sense, it became possible to imagine that certain companies had a pipeline to free Federal reserve cash. Picture many hundreds of billions being looted by Fed connected insiders, and that the quickest way to "launder" that money was to run it through a high flying stock, making it come out looking like stock market gains. Time will tell if Tesla, Amazon, and a few others were used in this manner.

Chapter 26

Fake Information Is Job #1...For Farming Humans

<u>This Chapter is about:</u> Misinformation simply pays much more. Trick #18 for Farming Humans.

<u>It is important because:</u> To protect yourself in today's world, one must become an expert on misinformation tactics and tricks.

Agnotology
You may have heard of <u>epistemology</u>, the study of knowledge. This field helps define what we know and why we know it. On the flip side of this is <u>agnotology</u>, or the study of the deliberate spread of ignorance. It comes from "agnosis", the Greek word for ignorance or 'not knowing', and "ontology", the branch of philosophy which deals with the nature of being.

> At risk of repeating...Agnotology is the study of willful acts to spread confusion and deceit, usually to unduly influence the public, often in order to sell a product or win favor.
> https://philpapers.org/archive/PROATM.pdf

> "Doubt is our product."
>
> Agnotology is more than the study of what we don't know; it's also the study of why we are not supposed to know it. One of its more important aspects is revealing how people, usually those in business or power, use ignorance as a strategic tool to hide or divert attention from societal problems in which they have a vested interest.   Misinformation has now become an infodemic.
>
> A perfect example is the tobacco industry's dissemination of reports that continuously questioned the link between smoking and cancer. As one tobacco employee famously stated, "Doubt is our product."

Agnotology is a term created by Robert N. Proctor in a book titled, AGNOTOLOGY, The Making and Unmaking of Ignorance.

Robert N. Proctor is Professor of the History of Science at Stanford University and the author of The Nazi War on Cancer (1999) and Cancer Wars: How Politics Shapes What We Know and Don't Know (1995).

The world is over-run with false information. This is remarkable in an age where humans are at our highest-ever levels of technological, scientific and supposed mental progress.

What if the more technology and appliances of mass *distraction* we carry in our hands, the less focused on what is real we become? The less informed and more easily fooled we are? What if technology is making us dumbed down sensation-seekers in critical ways?

Perhaps the false can no longer be separated from the truth… in a world where stimulation and distraction is King.

To those whose business is the spreading of falsehoods, lies and fake information, they would prefer to dismiss the field of Agnotology with a blanket label of "conspiracy theorists". Such slurs are themselves a good example of "willful acts to spread confusion and deceit."

Proctor cites as his prime example of the deliberate production of ignorance, the tobacco industry's advertising campaign to cause doubt about the cancer effects of tobacco use. Under the banner of science, the industry pumped out research about everything except tobacco hazards to exploit public uncertainty.

Undue influence is a term to describe persons who take advantage of power over other persons. This inequity in power between the parties can *destroy or impair* one party's consent as they are unable to freely exercise their independent will. Advertising, politics, finance…all profit from finding ways to unduly influence the public.

Farming humans using undue influence causes financial hardship to millions of people. Perhaps more like billions.

What are other words for financial hardship?

SYNONYMS. privation, deprivation, destitution, poverty, austerity, penury, want, need, neediness, beggary, impecuniousness, impecuniosity, misfortune, distress, suffering, affliction, trouble, pain, misery, wretchedness, tribulation, adversity, disaster, ruin, ruination, calamity.

These are the visible effects of farming humans from my own understanding, and observations.

You may have experienced something entirely different, even if you lived in the same place, during the same time, however that does not make either of our observations right or wrong. We may simply be seeing our own unique sources of information.

We may share different lives, experiences, and different conditions. We not only _cannot see_ things the same way, we literally cannot have seen the same things. And even if we were to see exactly the same thing, our individual mental conditionings would cause us to have different _interpretations and understandings of the very same experience._

I see a homeless person and I see a victim of a rigged and unfair system…whereas a person standing next to me might say, "look at that lazy drug addict…why doesn't he just get a job". Who is right? Who is to say?

I say the following after working twenty years inside the financial system:

The secret super-power of powerful abusers is in their ability to keep their abuses secret.

There are two very distinct subsets of Organized Crime. One appears in the news, and one is protected by being deliberately omitted from the news. Which one is more dangerous to you?

One is made visible and even inflated or sensationalized for media ratings, while the other is invisible, and ignored, for quid pro quo.

The "Unique Violence of White Collar Crime", is when professional level organized crime is one of the better concealed secrets on the planet. It is a kind of free-crime upon society which is almost never prosecuted. It is even better concealed than abuses by churches over the years, although they too, were experts at keeping secrets.

Are suffering people like this child (or his family) be the *real problem in our world today*, or could they be a *result* of the problem? I hope to convince people to not always blame the vulnerable for the crimes of the truly guilty, the rich and powerful.

And what if beyond Agnotology, is something known as Agnotology 2.0?

Agnotology too, is transforming. Today, the goal may no longer be to simply create ignorance, because there seems less concern in society to determine the validity of knowledge.

Under Agnotology 2.0, the concept of true or false becomes a moot point. It is only *public sensation* that counts. Public media leaders create an impact with whichever arguments they can muster based in whatever fictional data they wish to create.

In the past it took powerful people, billionaires or major corporations, to generate significant levels of doubt; now, with social media, anyone can provide counter-factual information to create doubt. For example, "alternative facts" was a new term that came along in 2017.

A good sign of society being farmed is when the news is filled daily with crisis after crisis, all man made (or made up), and they contain two constants: (1) Each one is intended to stir emotions of fear, hate, often to the point of violence, and (2) Each carefully hides the motivations and the secret games played by those seeking money, power and control over the public.

As we watch Donald Trump take on the most powerful position in the world, many of us are left asking how a man who has consistently lied to his public could get so far.
Some pundits are calling this the dawn of a new era. They say we now live in a post-fact or post-truth world. This is a time where the emphasis is not on coherence or rationality but on sensationalism, no matter the cost.

https://theconversation.com/scientists-have-a-word-for-studying-the-post-truth-world-agnotology-71542

Do some politicians have drug-like effects upon mass society?

If so, then this is yet another way to farm humans. A recent (2020) book called "Hacking Humans brings a valuable perspective on this topic. It is worth a look to understand why humans may be the easiest animals…to farm.

Chapter 27

Junk Data and Emotional Stimulation

This Chapter is about: Humans are overfed with data, stimulation and distraction, and not fed much true knowledge. This is Trick #19 for Farming Humans.

It is important because: The easiest person to con, is the person who thinks they are too smart to be conned. We are all victims since human gullibility is not self-revealing.

We all understand what junk food does to our bodies, but I do not hear much talk about what junk data is doing to our minds, and our society.

Speaking for myself, I can say for certain that "human stupidity is not self-revealing". A simple explanation for this is that our human senses are programmed to be vigilant and aware of danger. A long time ago we mistakenly assumed that we were not much of a danger to ourselves, and thus our instincts for survival became focused on *outside* dangers.

Humans don't observe ourselves very consciously, but we focus intently upon the actions of those around us. This creates huge blind spots in our self-knowledge and our behavior, which are invisible to us because of our constant focus on others.

With technology, it is also fair to say that humans are over-stimulated and easily addicted to distraction. Humans are being "dumbed down", and when you think about it, it looks quite intentional. Farming humans is easier if nine out of ten are getting their world-view by staring at an electronic screen…and thus being fed with algorithms of political and commercial distraction messages.

When combined with the known mental affects of poverty, which is found to reduce IQ levels of those who fall into poverty by about 14 points, it is possible to observe the dumbing down of North America in real time. It is like being witness to a train wreck, and watching it happen in slow motion. Add in the intentional mis-information, and political mind games and it is also like watching frogs being heated to a boil…in slow motion.

Or it is like winning the lottery, if you are a political or corporate entity with a desire to farm humans. It becomes easier to take advantage of people, because we humans mistakenly assume that we are smarter than those who came before us, with all the technology at our fingertips. The opposite is more likely, but just the "belief system" that we are smarter than any society that walked this planet, makes us easier victims for those who take advantage of what us humans do not know…about human nature.

Why Farming Humans is the easiest game in town.

Author and expert Maria Konnikova explains in 2 minutes, why incredibly smart people become victims of confidence games Maria Konnikova:

"We are all vulnerable to con artists (Feb 24, 2016) | Charlie Rose"

https://www.youtube.com/watch?v=KjIpYiT8kjQ

Today we "swim" in automatic, algorithmic feeds of specific information to each tech user, based upon whatever can stimulate the user…fear, anger, anxiety, hatred, love any emotion desired can be created, stimulated, tracked and capitalized upon.

We swim in this "derivative" information environment like a fish swims in water. Our children are being raised in this environment, and some will never imagine that there are other environments, or belief systems to live in. It would be like asking a young fish, "how's the water"? How would he even know what you were talking about if he has never known anything else?

Today, humans are being farmed by emotional distraction games and stimulation techniques that act below levels of our own awareness. Cambridge Analytica did this professionally using online information about each of us. So many data points are known about us that experts may know us better than we truly know ourselves.

Emotional triggers are used to stimulate the human tech user to shop, vote, protest, eat, to do whatever is desired by those who pay the algorithm creators.

We are being farmed electronically, economically, politically, and in ways which I cannot even imagine.

CEO Alexander Nix said Cambridge Analytica (CA) was involved in 44 US political races in 2014.

CA would collect data on voters using sources such as demographics, consumer behavior, internet activity, and other public and private sources. According to The Guardian, CA used psychological data derived from millions of Facebook users, largely without users' permission or knowledge. Another source of information was the "Cruz Crew" mobile app that tracked physical movements and contacts and according to the Associated Press, invaded personal data more than previous presidential campaign apps. (Wikipedia)

"Today in the United States we have somewhere close to _four or five thousand data points on every individual_ ... So we model the personality of every adult across the United States, some 230 million people."
— Alexander Nix, chief executive of Cambridge Analytica, October 2016.

In hidden camera interviews Cambridge Analytica sales agents boasted of being able to use thousands of data points on individuals, to predict which were not voters, and were members of special interest groups that could be aroused to action.

Whether they be Neo-Nazi groups, or any other special interest group, Cambridge knew precisely which emotional buttons could be pushed in certain individuals, to engage or to enrage them to action. The magic of Cambridge's work was in being able to "swing" an election by causing a small percentage of the population, those who usually would not vote, to come out in numbers and support the candidate desired by those who hired Cambridge. It is like an internet service where the precise information designed to trigger _just those certain people to action_, were directed at them. And it worked. It was far more effective than the "dog whistle" style of public messaging typically used to target voting subgroups.

Dog-whistle politics is political messaging employing coded language that appears to mean one thing to the general population but has an additional, different, or more specific resonance for a targeted subgroup. The analogy is to a dog whistle, whose ultrasonic tone is heard by dogs but inaudible to humans.

All that the powers above need do, is to create a fake "threat" to grab our attention, our emotions and energy. By causing us to focus fear or hate upon a common enemy (even a false one) it automatically gives us a group to "belong to".

"Belonging" to something is one of the strongest human emotional urges, one that we are all instinctually pulled to. Humans will do literally anything if it will allow them to "belong", to be liked, admired, respected, wanted or needed. To create an enemy, for a radical or extreme group is _like "giving candy to a baby"_. It is giving them something highly desired, in this case it is giving them something to belong to. Mere sensation. No facts are needed. Like a drug it plays on our emotional feelings, and that allows both the Hacking and the Farming of Humanity.

Recall that Agnotology 2.0 talks about not even having to get facts verified in the modern world, humans can now be controlled just by "sensation and storytelling"…the facts may now be irrelevant to humans. Just watch a few political rallies and see how much they resemble an old spiritual revival meeting…or a traveling wrestling show. You are watching instinctual tribalism in action. A mind game dressed up as intelligent individual thought.

Once we have "found" the common enemy to hate, or be in opposition towards, we then "believe" we know who the real enemy is, and that is a tremendous advantage to powers who manipulate humans. We even stop looking for who the true manipulators are once we are "convinced" of whom to fear, whom to hate. Another sale of another man-made belief system is complete. Sell enough man-made belief systems and you got yourself a way to farm humans.

The bedside reading of one of Canada's more predatory Prime Minister's included the book "The Prince", by Machiavelli.

Someone Machiavellian is sneaky, cunning, and lacking a moral code. The word comes from the Italian philosopher Niccolò Machiavelli, who wrote the political treatise "The Prince" in the 1500s. It encouraged "the end justifies the means" behavior, especially among politicians.

"An effective prince who wants to stay in power must be willing to put virtue (traits such as generosity, loyalty, honesty, and mercy) aside when necessary in order to instill fear in both his enemies and his followers, as fear generates respect. Characterized by subtle or unscrupulous cunning, deception, expediency, or dishonesty."

I read "Lord of the Flies" in high school, and although I did not fully appreciate it at the time, today I am grateful. That book gave me advance warning about the human instincts for tribalism, whether it be sports-tribalism, political-tribalism or schoolyard-bully-tribalism. The easiest way to dumb down an entire race, is to show them a team, religion, enemy or opponent that they can pretend to be better than, angry about, or threatened by. You can own some humans for life if you can keep the hidden instincts of tribalism fueled, and the beauty is, humans will never look at themselves closely enough to admit they are being driven by tribal instincts, not intellect. We humans are almost "self-hacking" in that regard.

Fear trumps intelligence almost every time.

Fear (and anger, hate etc) are man-made chemicals which act in the brain, (cortisol, adrenaline etc) and intelligence is mere thought processing in the brain.

Emotions are chemical. Thought is electrical.

Chemical triggers to the brain are may times more powerful motivators than mere electrical impulses. (think jealousy or murderous rage for example)

Chemicals make people lose their minds...hence fear and other similar emotions trumps intelligence. This is also how to hack and to farm humans. Give them something to hate, to be afraid of, or to think of as an enemy, and you have even sane, intelligent people, in palm of your hand.

Again, I wonder if some politicians have figured out how to use fear and hate to obtain drug-like effects upon mass society?

Internet Neutrality and Misinformation

Spreading false information is not good for society, but works great for political and economic predators. Net Neutrality is another example we can use to learn about the spread of misinformation today.

The internet is a system of public infrastructure, a series of connections that can be used by everyone, like our national highways. All traffic is equally welcome to travel those public highways, and this benefits everyone in the country.

Net neutrality is the idea that all internet traffic should be treated the same, with no internet service provider (ISP) having the power to favor one information source over another by blocking, throttling, or any means of paid prioritization. This makes net neutrality a crucial aspect in helping this public infrastructure be made fairly available to all.

Net neutrality levels out the playing field of all information, so the false cannot hide the truth. So that money cannot buy (or bury) the truth in any matter.

Net neutrality is about whether or not all information has access to the internet. Choking off facts or truth, in favor of lies and sensational information is something that would benefit those interested in controlling and farming humans.

For the benefit of the American public, the Obama administration put government policies in place that assured that Americans access to the information on the internet would not be abused in any way by those who seek to spread lies.

In the next US administration, those protections for fair access to all information on the net were quickly cancelled.

Without net neutrality, the information which first reaches your screens, may be information that is being sponsored, rather than the truth, or information of value. It may even be information designed to trigger a certain emotion or sensation in you, like Cambridge Analytica did in 2017. Since more money can be made by fooling people, our leaders have now made it legal to buy the right to more easily fool people.

Without net neutrality, truth, news and accurate information can be hidden, slowed or overpowered by faster traffic, fake or commercially purchased messaging. It allows freedom of information to be replaced with a 1990's style of Soviet-like propaganda or misinformation. It is how societies die, and it is now law in the United States. It is another essential ingredient in dumbing down the humans in a society to make them easier to farm.

The deliberate spread of mis-information is easier if access of information on the internet can be commercialized, or sold to the highest bidder.

On December 14, 2017, the Federal Communications Commission (FCC) voted in favor of repealing these policies, 3–2, along party lines, as the 2015 vote had occurred. ... On June 11, 2018, the repeal of the FCC's rules took effect, ending network neutrality regulation in the United States. (Trump era)

For more about easily conning humans, and hacking humans, read some of the work by Maria Konnikova "why humans are so easily conned".

Chapter 28

Fairness Doctrine, the media can now legally lie to you.

This Chapter is about: Elimination of a safe and sound news media is Farming Humans Trick #20

It is important because: Without a safe or honest media, any country can be taken advantage of by '90's Soviet-style dis-information and propaganda.

"...elimination of 83 regulations, including one of the agency's most famous: the Fairness Doctrine." Dylan Matthews, Washington Post Aug 23, 2011

On August 23, 2011, FCC chairman Julius Genachowski announced the elimination of 83 regulations, including one of the agency's most famous: the Fairness Doctrine.

The **fairness doctrine** of the United States Federal Communications Commission (FCC), introduced in 1949, was a policy that required the holders of broadcast licenses to both present controversial issues of public importance and to do so in a manner that was—in the FCC's view—honest, equitable, and balanced. The FCC eliminated the policy in 1987 and removed the rule that implemented the policy from the *Federal Register* in August 2011.

The First Amendment (US) does not permit government interference with the freedom of the press. If the press can make more money by lying or spreading propaganda, well...welcome to the Derivative Revolution. News no longer has to be the truth, but can be any derivative of truth that a special interest wishes you to believe.

As a child I recall visits to the U.S., where my family was met at the border by a smiling, welcoming, US border agent, dressed more like a national park ranger if memory serves me correctly. It gave the feeling that we were going to a great place when these border crossing experiences happened. Today I am reminded of crossings which have more of an "East Germany, 1980's paranoia", feel. The vibe of freedom, of confidence and happiness, seems to have been lost.

The fairness doctrine had two basic elements: It required broadcasters to devote airtime to discussing controversial matters of public interest, and air contrasting views regarding those matters. Stations were given discretion as to how to provide contrasting views: It could be done through news segments, public affairs shows, or editorials. The doctrine did not require equal time for opposing views but required that contrasting viewpoints be presented. The demise of this FCC rule has been considered by some to be a contributing factor for rising levels of party polarization and populism.

Populism:
Populism refers to a range of political stances that emphasize the idea of "the people" and often juxtapose this group against "the elite". The term developed in the 19th century and has been applied to various politicians, parties, and movements since that time, although has rarely been chosen as a self-description.

The First Amendment does not permit government interference with "the freedom of the press." What that freedom is, is among the great undefined terms in American jurisprudence. But its enduring strength is that few are willing to take the first step down the slippery slope of determining who is a journalist and who is not, and what constitutes good journalism and what does not. It's all protected, for good or ill.

An example from 1997 involves Jane Akre and Steve Wilson, TV journalists pressured by their employer, Tampa-based Fox affiliate WTVT, to alter a story on the use of recombinant bovine growth hormone (rBGH) in dairy production and its potential health risks to consumers. Akre and Wilson said they were ordered by Fox executives to change the story by inserting statements from rBGH manufacturer Monsanto that they knew to be false. They claimed that they were fired after refusing to do so and threatening to report the station to the FCC.

They sued for wrongful termination, asserting that their firing violated Florida's whistleblower protection statute. A jury ruled in Akre's favor, awarding her $425,000 in damages.
But a state appeals court overturned that decision in 2003, finding that the FCC's policy against "distorting the news" does not rise to the level of a law or regulation. In short, the court bought Fox's argument that there is no law to stop them from deliberately falsifying the news.

There is no licensing authority for journalists as there is for lawyers or doctors, but the Society of Professional Journalists puts forth a set of ethical standards, though it has no means to enforce them. First among them is: "Deliberate distortion is never permissible." It should go without saying, but there it is.

The rest of the standards touch on basic tenets of honesty (don't fabricate, mislead, deceive, silence opposing views), humanity (show compassion, respect and sensitivity to subjects who have undergone trying or traumatic events), and integrity (avoid conflicts of interest and disclose those that cannot be avoided).

That's not too much to ask, is it? Seek the truth as best you can determine it, go about it with candor and compassion, and do so "without fear or favor"—a phrase attributed to New York Times patriarch Adolph Ochs, conveying independence and impartiality.
It remains the controlling principle in most of the news media, but too often, editorial decisions are made that bring the entire profession into disrepute. And that harms not just the journalists, but the rest of us, too, as our discourse is steeped in distrust, cynicism and vitriol.

from https://www.washingtonpost.com/blogs/ezra-klein/post/every-thing-you-need-to-know-about-the-fairness-doctrine-in-one-post/2011/08/23/gIQAN8CXZJ_blog.html

Maybe Canada is onto something.

United States Federal Communications Commission (FCC) Fairness Doctrine
https://en.wikipedia.org/wiki/FCC_fairness_doctrine

It turns out that I am an accidentally trained NDT student. No, not "non-destructive testing", but "non-distractive testing". A friend showed me a book the other day titled "**Indistractable**: How to Control Your Attention and Choose Your Life".

As I work on this book about farming humans, it occurred to me that much of the human farming techniques that I write about, involve simple human distraction. It is as if we humans are like ten-week old kittens, and our unseen "owners" are using a laser pointer to get us to chase after the distraction. And chase we do…unconsciously, unknowingly, unceasingly.

Chapter 29
Government as Complication Creators

Public servants _milking systems better_...beneath a promise of _making systems better_. This political "bait and switch" is Farming Humans Trick #21.

This Chapter is about: Is government our servant, or master?

It is important because: It seems that between 1776 and 2020 they have pulled a bait and switch and reversed roles on the public.

In any first world country it seems as if the public is not often happy with their government. Whether it be the French with Yellow Vest protests, Hong Kong with democracy protests, Canada with their ongoing complaints that no matter which government we get, they seem to serve someone other than the people. I could add U.S,. Australia and others. No one seems to feel their government works for the public anymore.

I wonder if that is because it is no longer their government...could it be that government which is now a "partner in crime" with someone else? I keep seeing corporate and financial connections that seem to run many politicians, whenever I get a glimpse of what is going on behind the curtains.

If we paid close enough attention, it might be clear to more of the public that government in many developed countries is a bit of a ruse, a con, a deception? I am shocked at the signs which indicate that government is no longer about it's citizens. It is about big money getting together with power.

As the protest sign seen at Occupy Calgary, in 2011 said, "Politicians plus Corporations equals Fornications". It was a view that was ahead of it's time and seems to describe what is going on behind the backs of the public interest.

Two indicators of farming humans:

Dark Governments: Governments who pretend to serve the public, while secretly working for private or outside interests and influences beneath the surface.

Governance Betrayal: Selling out the public, while pretending to serve them.

Politicians can profit twice by acting as concealed corporate servants or "fifth columns" for corporate interests, while pretending to serve their public. Like the "fake advisors" in a previous chapter, governance betrayal is a criminal breach of the public trust, it just cannot be prosecuted in today's world. Justice, like gravity, is not allowed to flow upward towards the more powerful.

The professional creators of chaos, confusion and complication are the ones who tell proudly of their good motives, while hiding the true, bad motives behind layers of jargon and complexity.

Governments (whether pink, green, red or blue) now seem to be pathologically self-interested in re-election and self-preservation. Many politicians care more about power than public service. About what they can achieve with power, for themselves, rather than what can be done for the country. There are some good exceptions of persons who truly seek to serve others, but they are rare. Aspects of Greshams Law, (the bad drives out the good) have found their way into modern politics and we must find the "fix" to restore accountability in this arena.

Keep an eye on New Zealand for some positive modern examples of democracy. I think they might be leading the world in trying to serve humans and not simply farm them.

Chapter 30

North America Now Resembles The Soviet Union...of the 1990's

This Chapter is about: I watched the Soviet Union collapse in the 1990's. It then took decades before I mentally connected some of those dots, which taught me just how long it sometimes takes to see the big picture.

It is important because: Part of the picture that appeared over time was in the poverty and inequality that now appears in North America and other first world countries.

Similar financial failures, pension problems, poverty, addiction, hopelessness that were observed three decades ago in the Soviet Union, were starting to appear here. I recall the news media (1990's) reporting on the collapse of the USSR, and seeing people selling personal belongings in public markets. I watched as senior citizens were selling old shoes and personal items to obtain money.

The memory stayed with me since I was from a society where I had never seen such things in my life. When I was young and living in the prosperous west, I had no memory of such a thing as a "garage sale", or a public market of used goods.

Even a yard or moving sale does not register in my memory. Nor do I recall seeing an abandoned home in my city. I saw abandoned houses in movies, but not in real life. Then the century turned, and our western reality began to change.

Today, while we do have positive economic growth for some, there are many economic failure indicators in my country. They include people sleeping in the cold squalor of abandoned houses. Drugs, liquor stores, pawn shops, and payday lending stores have become a growth industry in the west, while productive industry is shuttered or moved to lower wage countries. The growth industry today is in "economic extraction", while real economic production is having a difficult time. "Financialization" seems to be the name of the game, and "economic extraction" is what that means, rather than economic production. Why build factories and produce goods if quicker money can be made by stripping companies instead. General Electric, Boeing, 3M, Sears, Toys R us, and so many others serve as examples of company stripping. Perhaps country stripping.

I have since watched Oliver Stone's "Putin interviews" and learned a bit more about what I had previously witnessed in the Soviet Union. Oscar-winning filmmaker Oliver Stone was granted unprecedented access to Vladimir Putin and Stone conducted more than a dozen interviews with the Russian president over a two-year period, with no topic off-limits.

One comment by Putin stood out for me in this series. It was when Putin described the collapse of the pension system in the Soviet Union. He spoke of people whose retirement income fell from the equivalent of $700 or $800 dollars per month, to closer to $40 per month. It struck me as similar to what I am hearing (about pension robbery taking place) in North America today.

The Putin Interviews - Oliver Stone Part 1 of 4
https://www.youtube.com/watch?v=QvlKSbYkTXI

Today, authors write about the theft of American's pensions. Wall Street wizards like Goldman Sachs and others have done a tremendous job of selling "crap" (their words) investments and snake oil to pensions, governments and others. Lawless Capitalism produces the greatest rewards to those who do the greatest harm. But don't worry, so does lawless Socialism or lawless Anything-ism. It is the lawless behavior that needs to be addressed, not a new "ism". If you don't believe me, ask an alcoholic.

Many banks and Investment dealers have become predators to their customers, while claiming to be their trusted servants and advisors. Full stop. Same with many other trusted professions and public servants.

In Canada, pension robbery is coming a bit closer to reality, with desperate politicians and investment bankers interested in the billions held inside public workers pensions, teachers pensions etc. Some of those political gangs have become interested in getting their hands, (or their friends hands), on those billions for their own political or financial ends. In the U.S., and elsewhere, clever investment bankers have been preying upon large pension funds for decades. Chris Tobe is a former pension fund trustee, and has written about his personal experience in the U.S. state of Kentucky.

"Kentucky Fried Pensions" is a book about the intentional pillage of pension funds by so-called investment advisors.

The book by Chris Tobe, a former trustee of the $14 billion Kentucky Retirement Systems and the first public pension whistleblower to file a complaint with the SEC's Office of the Whistleblower, focuses upon corruption at public pensions.

While Alicia Munnell's recent book "State and Local Pensions: What Now?" concentrates on the funding issues plaguing public pensions, Tobe says his book was inspired by the following quote from her:

"The issues confronting state and local pensions, while not trivial, are manageable. Well, maybe not in every case. In Illinois and possibly Kentucky, she says, "they should be hysterical."

Tobe establishes a link between corruption related to pension investments and corruption related to underfunding in Kentucky and Illinois. The central thesis is that pension cultures that are willing to look the other way regarding unsavory investment dealings will go along with bogus pension funding schemes as well.

Forbes article titled **Kentucky Fried Pensions** by Edward Siedle, Aug 8, 2013. Found at https://www.forbes.com/sites/edward-siedle/2013/08/08/kentucky-fried-pensions/#70e8bd064470

Chapter 31

Organized Professional Crime
Society's Secret Invisible...Secret

<u>This Chapter is about:</u>   Like a giant Aspen forest, the underground connections between professional criminals are invisible to the public. This is Farming Humans Trick #22.

<u>It is important because:</u>   What if the greatest undeclared social pandemic of modern times is hiding invisibly right in front of us? A pandemic of professional quid pro quo.

In recent years I have become aware of two new and interesting creatures, which turn out to be among the largest living organisms on the planet. They are hidden in plain sight, yet right in front of us every day. I think there is something I am supposed to learn from the discoveries.

The first invisible-giant you may know about because it is not a public secret.

Anyone passing through the San Juan Forest can observe giant aspen groves. Hikers, bikers or horseback riders who go slow can immerse themselves. The startling part is that hidden from sight, beneath the ground are billions of connected root fibers, that tie this Aspen forest into _one_ single co-operating and communicating organism, much like the human brain with its billions of connections. What an amazing discovery.

In a research capacity, Grant, who is a professor in the Ecology and Evolutionary Biology Department, has served as the resident expert for fall aspen tree colors. One of his most widely publicized research findings also involves the quaking aspen.

In the early 1990s, Grant and fellow CU-Boulder professors Jeffry Mitton and Yan Linhart published a paper in Nature magazine asserting that a particular aspen clone in Utah - that the team later dubbed Pando, for the Latin word "I spread" - deserved consideration for being the world's largest living organism.

Pando consists of nearly 50,000 tree trunks covering roughly 106 acres. Grant and his colleagues calculated that the aspen clone weighed in at about 13 million pounds, which would make it the most massive organism in the world known to date.

https://www.colorado.edu/today/2016/04/12/teaching-trees-reflecting-four-decades-cu-boulder

A second giant creature is also invisible to us, while sitting in plain sight.

Professional connections and quid pro quo's which engage in organized crime is also invisible to most humans as a co-operating entity. Instead it merely looks like millions of professionals, bankers, brokers, lawyers, judges, politicians, accountants, regulators, auditors and so on, going about their business and doing their jobs, independent of each other. Each promises to do a professional job of serving and protecting the public, while I can tell you from inside experience that the system, and one's place within the system is sometimes of greater importance than protection of the public. Not in all cases, but in enough to affect, or infect our society with very negative results.

Not many insiders can risk going against their own systems, their profession, or industry practices, even when those practices turn corrupt.

Such are the effects of tribalism, and offshoots of Gresham's Law. "The bad drives out the good" is one part of Gresham' Law that can corrupt any system. Codes of silence and human instincts of tribalism, prevent even ethical professionals from speaking out, when persons around them are making millions or billions by acting illegally. There is simply too much power behind billion dollar opportunities, to swim against the industry current.

Please do not take my word for this, but look into the topic of whistleblowers, those rare individuals who dare to speak out against their company or industry, when the public is being abused. It is a horrible thing to witness, when even professionals silence the truth at times. "Self" regulation is the free pass that allows the truth to be silenced to protect professional reputations, instead of protecting society.

Society has no way of seeing beneath the surface and knowing the connections, relationships and hidden opportunities beyond our view. These symbiotic connections could be seen as the "quid pro quo" that we hear about occasionally. We never know that beneath the surface, entire systems often involve quid pro quo between professions. There is a lot going on behind the robes and closed doors...when the deals are big enough to make a fortune on any one.

I spent two decades inside organizations whose unspoken, inner, private behavior was to get #RicherByCheating. The unwritten code of silence was orders of magnitude more valuable to the firm's profits than any written code of ethics. A majority of activity involved setting up relationships and quid pro quo's which ensure that cheating of the public would never be made public. (regulation backed by self regulation, backed by...) I now have decades of observation, both inside these firms and out, and yet I still find it hard to believe how easy it is.

It took more than ten years for me to even see what was going on beneath the surface in my own industry. By the time I noticed how investment customers being farmed, and I followed company codes of ethics (my cries of "WOLF"), rather than the codes of silence, I had no idea of the inner codes of silence. They were as invisible to me as the connected root systems of a giant forest.

Strict codes of silence were unwritten, and unspoken, but were adhered to more rigorously than were any written codes of ethics.

Imagine how long it will take the public to learn of systemic professional crime, if the connections are so well concealed. It was not that I misunderstood the codes of ethics, I did pass all the exams on them, but my mistake was in not knowing that the codes of ethics were mere window dressings to help *conceal* the abuse of clients...not to reveal them.

I am not saying that all professionals operate in an organized gang-like manner. I am saying that there are countless connections that are invisible to the public. Many of those hidden connections and relationships are working to take advantage of the very people that the professions are formed to serve. There is simply many times more money to be made this way...and there is little or no chance of getting caught, due to the connections.

White Collar organized crime, consists of professionals and public servants, politicians, corporate lawyers, corporations, bankers, accountants, and so on. It also includes the media that profits by helping hide systemic cheating of the public, gaining advertising dollars in return. The easiest money in the world is to be made by taking the easy route, and the easy route involves one of the largest invisible entities on earth.

The "Creature" of professional organized crime has not been studied or measured to my knowledge. There is little or no enthusiasm for investigating this giant thing that no one can see. That despite it being capable of doing more harm, and draining more GDP, prosperity, and hope from our societies than any other entity. Perhaps I am wrong, but I saw clear lessons and examples from a few decades in and around those gangs.

Farming humans is easier than taking candy from a trusting child.

My daughter might appreciate this 30 year old story that I connected one more dot on today. I used to take her out for popsicles or ice cream when she was little. She was a real walking-talking, amazing little person then, so it was fun to play "lets pretend" or other games with her.

Sometimes when I consumed my frozen treat a bit faster than her, I would offer to trade her larger ice cream cone for what was left of mine. It was part jest and part test, and she usually went along with the trade, offering to give me her bigger treat in exchange for my own. Such was her innocence at the time. But as hoped, she caught on quickly to her early lesson in deception and in life skills.

Now, years later, she still reminds me of her discovery that I was "conning" her out of her ice cream, and occasionally threatens to put me in a home. I also just now connected another dot to how Corporations and other giant entities work together to similarly farm the public. These giant entities have had a few hundred years to perfect their con games, while us humans just arrived, within all the social constructs already made before we arrived.

A wise man once told me that "whatever it is I am thinking of, was already rigged long before I was even born…"

We are like young fish when an old fish swims by and asks, "how's the water boys?". The young fish do not have enough experience to know even what the question means. Because they have never experienced anything other than water. Farming humans, is as easy as taking candy from innocent children, since it has the same tricks of the old and the wise pulling the wool over the eyes of the innocent.

It is those timeless corporate entities, using rigged laws and belief systems created by lawyers centuries ago, who seem to set up society so the corrupt will always win. They will always hold an unfair advantage over everyday humans. They have repealed the laws of poverty (for themselves), by rigging some of the systems of prosperity for themselves.

Update April 18th, 2020:

As I consider the multi-thousand-dollar corona-virus support payments to the public, verses the multi-trillion-dollar payments to banks, billionaires and artificial "persons", I realize they were running a similar deception-game on innocent people. They were making sure that they got over 80% of public relief first, and offering comparative "pennies" to the public to the tiny innocent public...somewhat like the ice cream con game I played with my daughter thirty years ago.

Thought experiment:

Everyone knows that we cannot repeal the laws of gravity for some people to give them a physical advantage over others.

We can however, using man-made "belief systems", relax laws of prosperity for certain people, and apply laws of poverty more heavily on others. Just get society to play, "Lets pretend..." and to go along with a uniquely-created game and uniquely-enforced system of beliefs. This is easy using the "professions" of politics, law and finance.

"Corporate persons" then gain an elevated status above the average man on the street. Then there are also professionals who operate through a professional corporation which may give them the benefits of "self" regulation and further benefits of corporate immunity. Twice elevated above the man on the street. Two superior powers, based on a simple game of "I have an idea, lets pretend that....".

Now toss in an **image of respectability** and an **aura of trust**, the two ingredients necessary in a con game. "Lets put our higher status people in robes, gowns or special business-suits, to set them apart from those we wish to direct...we will even use complexity or Latin to show how truly superior we are…they will trust us like they are innocent children."

That may be why farming humans today, is easier than taking popsicles or ice cream from a trusting child…it has less to do with serving or helping people and more to do with rigging the game. Rent seeking is another term for rigging the game, and we will cover that as well in this book.

Elford's Law: The higher in dollar value that crimes rise to, the lower the probability of police or prosecutor action.

At financial 'altitudes' of tens or hundreds of millions of dollars and above, a completely different system of justice takes control. A system of justice that is invisible to all who are outside that system.

Agnotologist Observation:

Codes of silence in any system, are <u>never written</u>, but <u>always</u> enforced.

Codes of ethics are <u>always written</u>, but most often never enforced. They are sometimes called "window dressing", (for appearances only).

Ingredients essential to Professional Organized Crime:

1.   "Self"-regulation protects each profession
2.   Corporate limited liability protects each corporation
3.   Corporate insulator effect "I didn't do it, my invisible friend did"
4.   Management insulator effect (replace a manager and continue the crime spree)
5.   Professional and political quid pro quo
6.   Ignored by government prosecutors
7.   Ignored by police
8.   Ignored by government regulators

> "Quid pro quo"
> What is the difference between a quid pro quo and a bribe?
>
> Quid pro quo simply means something for something. It can be perfectly legal and above board. Bribes are a type of quid pro quo which ignores legal/moral boundaries.   Quora.com

Perhaps we should stop pretending that professionals, politicians and men in suits are not just like every other human when they commit crimes? Perhaps we should begin to hold them to account, rather than letting them "police" themselves.

Existential Comics
@existentialcoms

America is a country where billionaires find it cheaper to finance elections to get people in who will cut their taxes than to just pay the taxes. This is called democracy, apparently.

8:17 PM · 2/8/19 ·

Chapter 32

OCCUPY 2011
"Land of the Free"…(unless you peacefully assemble:)

<u>This Chapter is about:</u> Distractions and public silence are needed to keep public attention focused away from the games being played upon society. Trick #23 for Farming Humans is a militarized police used to serve and protect power and silence people.

<u>It is important because:</u> If public attention is silenced by violence, we are not allowed spot the harmful games which are played on the public.

Systemic literacy is an awareness of the less visible games being <u>played upon us</u>, and not be lost in the games used <u>to confuse or distract us</u>.

What if you and I are like every other human in the world and any ten week old kitten, mostly unaware or unconscious of our own human instincts, thoughts, emotions and triggers? What if we are being "played", stimulated and distracted in order that we might not even see the real game. The game that billionaires and some governments play. As Yuval Noah Harari states, we have the technology today so that humans are now "hackable animals".

Hacking Humans - Yuval Noah Harari
"We are now hackable animals", from his latest book, "21 Lessons for the 21st Century."
www.ynharari.com › ynh-on-impact-theory

Occupy 2011 (Occupy Wall Street protests for those who missed it) was a glimpse of North Americans trying to understand what is actually going on, to try and visualize the game beneath the surface.

See YouTube: "CNN Explains: The Occupy movement" for a 2 minute clip to explain the 2011 Occupy protest movement.

If you go back a bit further, protests in the '80's and '90's against the World Trade Organization (WTO) are worth studying as well. Sadly I was immersed in the financial industry then and was blindly unaware of what was going on. I was literally watching the wrong game at the time. Anyone who looks back might discover well informed people warning us of the signs of farming humans.

Occupy 2011 (or "Occupy Wall Street") began after banks almost collapsed from their own investment gambling, and were "rewarded" with taxpayer-funded money. Some people realized that something was very wrong in our social and economic systems. Few knew _what_ was wrong, but people demanded answers. Americans had just been robbed by Trillions of dollars and the robbers were rewarded and paid bonus's at public expense. Peaceful protestors received pepper spray to the face by the forces employed to aid…in the farming of humans.

It is now early 2020 as I write this, and I am amazed at how resilient the French (Yellow Vest) protesters are, how long they have stood their ground, and how much world attention they are getting.

The protests began on November 17, 2018, and attracted more than 300,000 people across France with protesters constructing barricades and blocking roads. It is now early 2020 and the protests continue. I believe they are questioning the same invisible creature that "Occupy Wall Street" was, but like giant groves of aspen trees, the organism is not visible to most of the public yet.

This CNN News clip says a lot about French protests in a 55 second message:
"France Protests Bank-Caused Debt-Slavery Dec 2018, 55 sec"
https://www.youtube.com/watch?v=nao0S17iplw)

Switching briefly to Hong Kong Democracy protests (2019, 2020), they had massive protests and some social unrest, until a fortunately-timed virus came along and put an end to it.
It reminded me a bit of that time the CIA was found to have used torture, like a third world dictator would….and poof, within a few days the entire news story was wiped from existence by a story about North Korea.
Hol-
ly-

wood
had a film coming out which portrayed comedic attempts to assassinate the leader of North Korea, and what do you know…all of a sudden, the North Korean leader was rumored to be planning retaliation against the film in some way. I cannot make this stuff up, but I can luckily still remember some elements of it. POOF! The story of the CIA using torture disappears…removed from eyes, the TV's, and the minds of millions of people in one day.

The purpose of this illustration is to shine a light into how easily we humans are hacked, distracted, diverted, and to serve as a reminder that our human attention spans are often as short as kittens chasing laser pointers. This applies to myself. I am no better than the next guy during a well played public distraction.

The Interview is a 2014 American action comedy film co-produced and directed by Seth Rogen and Evan Goldberg in their second directorial work, following *This Is the End* (2013). The screenplay was written by Dan Sterling, based on a story he co-wrote with Rogen and Goldberg. The film stars Rogen and James Franco as journalists who set up an interview with North Korean leader Kim Jong-un (Randall Park), and are then recruited by the CIA to assassinate him. The film is heavily inspired by a 2012 *Vice* documentary.In June 2014, The Guardian reported that the film had "touched a nerve" within the North Korean government, as they are "notoriously paranoid about perceived threats to their safety."

The Korean Central News Agency (KCNA), the state news agency of North Korea, reported that their government promised "stern" and "merciless" retaliation if the film was released. KCNA said that the release of a film portraying the assassination of the North Korean leader would not be allowed and it would be considered the "most blatant act of terrorism and war.
Wikipedia

What a great stroke of "publicity luck" for the movie. What a great bit of "timing luck" to take the public focus away from the "CIA as Torturer" story. What a huge bit of "media luck" to come across such a newsworthy story to share with the public. All happening at the same time, with all parties involved benefitting so well, just coincidence right? Judge for yourself, the jury is still out, I have no opinion but the timing was hilariously perfect. Even funnier than the movie.

That is how easy it is to farm humans, just keep the laser pointer moving. Humans are instinctually driven to give enormous amounts of mental attention to anything that "moves". Out of the billion things hitting our senses each day, the moving "thing" is given the greatest significance in our nervous systems. We are all easy marks for something "new", and anything "in motion".

Canadian lawyer Rocco Galati has some profound things to say about those who shout "conspiracy". They are often labeled "Conspiracy theorists" by way of throwing a negative, blanket label on those who question strange coincidences.

Mr. Galati suggests that perhaps those who use the label "conspiracy theorist" might be referred to as "Coincidence Theorists". He defined "Coincidence Theorists" as those who realize that several conditions often combine to create a very unusual outcome, but prefer to label those things as "pure coincidence". After all, he says, conspiracy is a criminal offense, and so anyone committing crimes of conspiracy, needs a blanket label to throw upon those who spot their crimes…a derogatory label. Hence "conspiracy theorist".

Readers will do themselves a favor if they discover a great writer, Mark Manson, author of the Subtle Art of Not Giving A F*ck, for a better understanding of what media is doing to aid in the farming of humans.

WHY YOU SHOULD QUIT THE NEWS

"I'm going to argue that the news doesn't just seem to be horrible, in its current form it is horrible. It is actively damaging our culture. And most of what we blame on social media or the internet—the upticks in stress, anxiety, pessimism, and polarization—is misplaced. News media is the true culprit."
https://markmanson.net/why-you-should-quit-the-news?utm_campaign=mmnet-newsletter-202003-01-20&utm_medium=email&utm_source=mmnet-newsletter&utm_content=read-why-you-should-quit-the-news

---

Chapter 33

Justice Systems?...Or "Just Us"?

<u>This Chapter is about:</u>   Why are there no prosecutions of the "professional organized crimes" of politicians, professionals etc?

<u>It is important because:</u>   If justice is not applied to some persons, but applied to others, then it is even legitimate, or some kind of power or control game? Farming Humans Trick #24.

There is statistically zero criminal enforcement against politically connected persons or corporations, and very little serious civil pursuit against banks. As some commentators have pointed out, when a bank cheats billions from the public, the most they can expect to happen is perhaps a small fine of 10% of their ill gotten gains, and that only happens once in a political blue moon. Corporations get to keep most of what they gain by way of professional organized crime, due to the miracles of "self" regulation.

No prosecutor in the land appears to have the freedom, or the courage to litigate against organized corporate crime. They know the case is not winnable when the justice system has connections to so many of the players. What do they know about underground quid pro quo connections, that the public does not know?

I hesitate to put a number on the dollar value of crime, above which no pursuit, criminal or civil is possible, but experience suggests that anything over $100 million dollars is untouchable. At $100 Million give or take a wide margin, it seems more like crime is something to be protected, and not something to be prosecuted. If those words seem hyperbolic, I understand. It is just my experience.

Corporate law firms seem able to earn more money by protecting our richest crimes, than anyone could ever earn by prosecuting them. My city of 100,000 people spends $40 million dollars on our police department to fight crime and keep the public safe. I am impressed with how well they do in a world where street crime seems to be increasing exponentially. There is an obvious economic relationship between the amount of "free crime" at the top of the economic food chain, and the increases in poverty, hopelessness addiction and street crime at the bottom. The police are doing a great job (on the streets) in my view. If memory serves me they responded to 35,000 calls in one year with their $40 million dollar budget.

However, the public must know that they (police) rarely respond or get involved in high value economic crime, and often they tell victims of million dollar crimes, that their complaint is a "civil matter" and should be dealt with in the civil courts. They do a great job at the level of street safety and property protection, but at most crimes over a certain financial level, or complexity, they defer to others. Police do not appear to function in government buildings and office suites, like they do in the streets.

My government has offices for high value economic crimes. These are commercial crime police units called the RCMP Integrated Markets Enforcement Teams. (RCMP IMET) By some coincidence they also operate on a budget in the neighborhood of $40 Million dollars...but $40 Million is what they have for the protection of the entire country of Canada. They handle perhaps a dozen cases a year, and we rarely hear of a successful prosecution. I believe it is intentional. No person power finds it wise...to investigate persons in power.

Yes, the entire country's elite corporate crime protection funding budget is similar to a city police force of one smaller city. One conclusion could be that the highest value economic crimes in the land, those done by bankers, lawyers, offshore money launderers, tax evaders and so on, are not something that authorities wish to police. The amounts drained (or gained?) from Canada by political, corporate and billionaire class crimes, are by my estimates, greater than all other measured criminal acts in the land. And yet, the powers that be police small crimes, while making almost zero attempt to police professional crime in office towers. There appear to be two sets of public protection policies, one for crime in the streets, and another for crime in the suites. Or perhaps there are different classes of justice for different classes of people. One effectively enforced justice system for the public, and a "gentleman's club" justice system for the influential and the elite.

In my search for truth at the top of the economic food chain, I have testified in four government or parliamentary committees, and in each case the result of all witness testimony and public news coverage into billion dollar systemic crimes was...nothing. No changes, no new protective laws, no effective structural change.

Correction...one government committee after the collapse of 2008 mortgage markets and the illegal sale of non-rated financial instruments did alter the law in one aspect...it eliminated jail sentences for bankers or "public markets participants" who were caught dealing fraudulently.

It must also be noted, that the change was already written, by lawyers, in advance of the committee meetings and any testimony from witnesses. The banks were able to amend laws and remove all threat of jail terms for financial market fraud, for bankers ("public markets" fraud was removed) and they were able to have this *done before the parliamentary committee even began its hearings* on the subject.

This is how efficiently the powerful can farm humans. I thought the government was investigating the banks, and I discover that it is not the government in charge at all, but the banks.

Meetings From 40th Parliament, 2nd Session
Bill C-52, An Act to amend the Criminal Code (sentencing for fraud) https://www.ourcommons.ca/Committees/en/JUST/Meetings?parl=40&session=2

That is just one example of what I have seen on my personal journey into professional white collar gangs, and organized criminality. It ties in with the theme of how to farm humans....that and the fact that many Canadian Ministers of Finance seem to be either former financial industry persons, and/or have been found to have significant holdings in offshore tax havens. The latest example being Finance Minister Bill Morneau, whose company was found among the clients involved in the Panama Papers. A book could probably be written about the history of Canadian Finance Ministers alone, they share so many common roots, much like groves of Aspen...

> Please forgive this repeat of <u>Elford's Law:</u> The higher in dollar value that crimes achieve, the lower the probability of police or prosecutor action.
>
> At financial altitudes of tens or hundreds of millions of dollars and above, an un-written system of justice takes over the controls. This system of justice is invisible to persons not inside the system.

Petty criminals are to be pursued with flash grenades and SWAT teams, with TV camera's rolling if possible, while at levels around $100 Million, the enforcement is usually nothing. Zip. Nada. Silence. No cameras, no media. Perhaps some private phone calls between political leaders to put pressure on Attorney Generals or Ministers to stop pursuing the case.

I have observed that crimes near or above $100 Million dollars are things to be "divvied up", and rarely, if ever prosecuted.

At higher dollar amounts, or higher status perpetrators, unseen systemic rewards seem to kick in which are more interested in protection of these "higher status" crimes or criminal actors. I attribute this to the hidden roots, connections and quid pro quos which come to the aid of people who commit hundred million dollar crimes. The Boston Globe Spotlight team observed trying to uncover powerful abusers in some of their stories. (The academy award winning film "Spotlight" is a example of how this works.)

Crime and tax evasion etc, are a free game for the richest while the poor are hunted down...by helicopter if necessary.
There is a tremendous ability to farm humans, when those who climb in status, benefit by being above rules and laws that apply to the rest of the population. It is strange to witness forces of justice, which one thinks apply like "gravity" to all, be ignored over and over depending upon the importance, power or influence of the criminals.

Government Justice Departments in many countries publish cost estimates on the value of criminal acts.
Even Gang and Organized Crime is information is published in North America by governments.

<u>High Status Crime by Professionals and Public Servants is not even measured in my</u> country. It is counted in exactly the same manner as abuses by the world's most powerful abusers...*which is to say it is not counted.* It is taboo... forbidden to talk about. That should tell you just how important this area is.

Chapter 34

Auditors "Breaking Bad"

<u>This Chapter is about:</u>   Public Corporation accounting can now be cooked as easily as making Meth in a motorhome…in the style of "Breaking Bad". Farming Humans Trick #25.

<u>It is important because:</u> It allows a "Paint by Numbers" falsified pictures of reality. Investors take heed.

"I would not hire you to audit the contents of my fridge"!!

British MP addresses KPMG, during UK Parliamentary hearings into bankruptcy of firm (Carillion) that KPMG gave clean financial bill of health just six months prior to going under.

Nothing can be depended upon, when corporations can purchase whatever financial number needed to show on a financial state-ment. Today, fraudulent accounting audits and letters of creditwor-thiness are bought and sold between audit firms and corporations. Yet society depends upon the accuracy of financial information to support companies, jobs, pensions, and investment.

I have a lot of respect for Dr. Al Rosen. He is a former accounting professor, one of the most reputable forensic accountants in North America. Dr. Rosen has consulted or given independent opinions on over 1,000 litigation-related engagements. In recent years he has written two books, which have sounded alarm bells about the state of the accounting profession, but the profession makes more money by not heeding his warnings. What concerns him should concern us all.

His first book was titled "Swindlers" and went into detail about how easy it is to financially dupe investors in Canada and the U.S. His book gave examples from cases he has handled in his career. His second book "Easy Prey Investors" is also a must read for anyone investing in Canada or the U.S. In it he reveals the tricks and traps of the accounting industry that no others in the industry have the courage or the moral freedom to voice.

The story below, from the UK, gives a snapshot and a link to the kind of accounting fraud that Dr. Al Rosen has long been warning us about.

January 15, 2018
On Monday, Carillion, the U.K.'s second-largest construction company, announced that it would go into compulsory liquidation.

Carillion is a construction company, it also provides facilities management and maintenance services such as cleaning and catering in the U.K.'s National Health Service hospitals, providing meals in 900 schools, and maintaining prisons. It holds a number of government contracts, including for the construction of a high-speed rail link and for the maintenance of roads.

43,000 employees worldwide, 20,000 work in the U.K.; the company also has a significant presence in the Middle East and Canada. The company has built iconic buildings in the U.K. and abroad, including the Tate Modern in London and the Grand Mosque in Oman. It is also responsible for the revitalization of Toronto's Union Station.

MPs have singled out a number of parties who played a role in the demise of outsourcing firm Carillion, naming both groups and individuals in their report .
The politicians – from a joint inquiry by the Business, Energy and Industrial Strategy Committee and Work and Pensions Committee – said the collapse of Carillion was a "story of recklessness, hubris and greed" and pulled no punches in their findings as to what led to the firm's failure, which put 20,000 jobs at risk.

Carillion's board bears the brunt of the responsibility, the report found, but there were others involved in the behaviour that ultimately pushed the company over the edge.

https://www.independent.co.uk/news/business/analysis-and-features/carillion-collapse-latest-who-responsible-richard-adam-howson-philip-green-mp-report-a8353921.html

KPMG audited Carillion's accounts for the entire 19 years of its existence, a relationship that made the accounting firm £29m. The committee noted that KPMG never qualified its audit opinion, "instead signing off the figures put in front of them by the company's directors".

MPs said: "In failing to exercise – and voice – professional scepticism towards Carillion's aggressive accounting judgements, KPMG was complicit in them. It should take its own share of responsibility for the consequences."

KPMG was not the only audit firm to get a mention in the report. Deloitte was responsible for advising Carillion's board on risk management and financial controls, and MPs found the firm was "either unable to identify effectively to the board the risks associated with their business practices, unwilling to do so, or too readily ignored them".

The committee also highlighted Ernst and Young's (EY) role in advising the company on how to make £123m in cost savings, which did not happen – but the firm was still paid £10.8m for its efforts.

EY was not alone in its position as an ineffectual adviser. The report states: "By the end, a whole suite of advisers, including an array of law firms, were squeezing fee income out of what remained of the company." Slaughter and May, Lazard and Morgan Stanley were all named in the document.

KPMG, the auditing firm that gave Carillion a clean bill of health, has reported a leap in profits that will result in the average pay of its 635 partners soaring from £519,000 to more than £600,000 each.
Only months after KPMG was accused by MPs of being part of a "cosy club" and "complicit" in the run-up to the collapse of the construction and government outsourcing company, the accountancy group reported an 8% rise in revenue to £2.3bn in the 12 months to 30 September. Profits surged 18% to £365m.

The Guardian

Earning $600,000 each, for 635 accounting firm partners is pretty easy money for playing paint by financial numbers. How much money could you make if you could pay your own self-regulators to police your behavior, while the outside world had to answer to real laws, real police officers and public courts?

Self regulation pays so very well, just not for the society we live in. It grants special privilege and exemption from law, more often than it protects the public. Professional self regulation should be considered a common theme of some of the greatest crimes against society.

From earlier in the research for this book comes this quote from a former Royal Canadian Mounted Police (RCMP) money laundering expert:

"......the Canadian Bar Association is probably the most powerful criminal organization in Canada..."
Former RCMP Inspector Bill Majcher,

See Youtube Video titled: *"France is Lost, The Fix is In: Gerald Celente & RCMP Inspector Bill Majcher" (1:20:00 on video)*

Another accounting professor who has gained international reputation for speaking truth is Professor Prem Sikka.

Prem Sikka is a British accountant and academic. He holds the position of Professor of Accounting at the University of Sheffield, and is Emeritus Professor of Accounting at the University of Essex.

His consistent writing about accounting and audit irregularities in the UK, is a valuable voice for society, that should be listened to, for countries interested in knowing how professional organized gangs loot the public.

But what power would care to look...when they can profit instead?

Chapter 35   2020

Destroying the planet for bits of paper.

<u>This Chapter is about:</u> Paper money is almost infinite. The planet is not. Farming Humans Trick #26.

<u>It is important because:</u>   To print near infinite "promises of wealth", in exchange for the finite wealth of the planet, is to destroy the planet. There is simply not enough "planet" to trade for "infinite promises".

Examples:
Burning the Amazon.
Feeding our garbage to all the marine life in the ocean.
Chemical spraying to destroy entire forests.

The herbicide Glyphosate is primarily used in agriculture, but it is also used in the forestry industry to kill deciduous trees — such as maple, oak, and birch — in order to allow trees used for pulp to flourish. Glyphosate spraying of Aspen forests seems particularly wrong to me now that I realize that such forests are among the largest living things on the planet. Same for dumping trillions of tons of waste and garbage into the Oceans.

I don't just dream of helping the environment. I dream of helping multiple environments.

1. I dream of seeing our natural environment allowed to survive and thrive.
2. I dream of seeing our financial environment able to survive and allow more people to prosper.
3. I dream of seeing social and political environments able to survive and thrive. This means freedom to not be coerced or corralled into economic traps, or rigged belief systems designed to benefit a small number of older, richer, whiter men.
4. I believe all these are connected, and all are at risk.

Farming Humans is about how to use cheating to the detriment of the planet and everything on it, in pursuit of bits of paper that we call money. The cheating allows clever men to create, and control most or all of that paper. This effectively gives a few clever (or sociopathic) men control over most of the wealth of the planet.

Bits of paper can be created infinitely. The earth can not. When I do the math, there appears to be no restraining or limiting factor which prevents our environment from being used or destroyed for someones private wealth. Any fool can make a Billion dollars by choosing to disregard the costs to the shared environment. However it involves a theft from everyone, when one man's selfish acts can destroy society's shared and common resources. There are no acting systems of law or protection for these crimes.

The environment has always been something to harvest or to destroy for those bits of paper. Recalling that one definition of corruption is the use of public power or assets for private gain…and it occurs to me that our shared environment should be lawfully considered as much of a public asset as anything else that fits that definition.

1. *What is the most important living thing on the planet?*

SCIENCE-ANDINFO.BLOGSPOT.COM

The Bee Is Declared The Most Important Living Being On The Planet

2. *What is one of the most dangerous living things on the planet?*
What if it is the *Corporation*?

Which one (a bee or a corporation) is a living, valuable, autonomous living thing, and which is a lawyer-created, paper based, belief system? A human derivative, if you will allow that label.

Which one grows stronger, while the other is being killed off in an addictive pursuit of more?

Which one produces life, benefitting what it touches, and which destroys life, in pursuit of tiny bits of paper?

Consider the image of one tiny creature working tirelessly and selfishly to carry the load for others, while also serving incalculable benefits in nature.

Economic Importance of Pollinators:

Insect pollination is integral to food security in the United States. Honey bees enable the production of at least 90 commercially grown crops in North America. Globally, 87 of the leading 115 food crops evaluated are dependent on animal pollinators, contributing 35% of global food production.

Pollinators contribute more than 24 billion dollars to the United States economy, of which honey bees account for more than 15 billion dollars through their vital role in keeping fruits, nuts, and vegetables in our diets.

Native wild pollinators, such as bumble bees and alfalfa leaf-cutter bees, also contribute substantially to the domestic economy. In 2009, the crop benefits from native insect pollination in the United States were valued at more than 9 billion dollars.

Source: The White House, Office of the Press Secretary
June 20, 2014

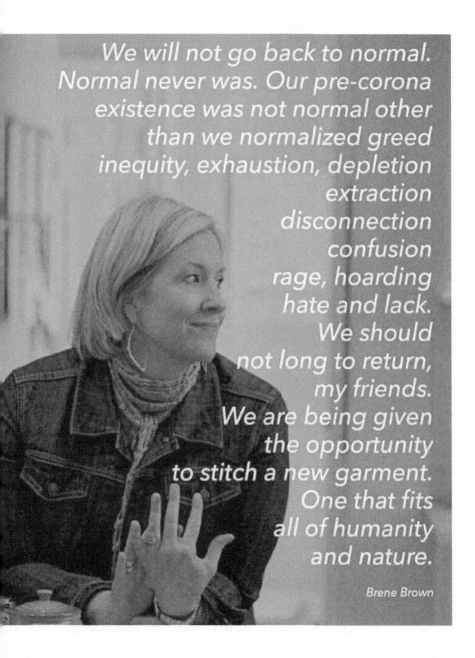

We will not go back to normal.
Normal never was. Our pre-corona
existence was not normal other
than we normalized greed
inequity, exhaustion, depletion
extraction
disconnection
confusion
rage, hoarding
hate and lack.
We should
not long to return,
my friends.
We are being given
the opportunity
to stitch a new garment.
One that fits
all of humanity
and nature.

Brene Brown

We don't need more cameras pointed at citizens. We need more cameras pointed at politicians

Chapter 36
Spy Industry, watching the wrong game...

This Chapter is about: Why are public servants listening to the public's telephone conversations? Trick # 27 for Farming Humans

It is important because: Since the public pays public servants and they serve the public, shouldn't the public be monitoring the servants instead of the other way around?

All spying eyes and ears seem to be directed upon the public, in a false game of "protecting" society. In reality, those in power are protecting themselves from being held accountable and responsible to the public. They invent crisis after crisis to justify increased power for themselves. This should tell us who the masters truly are, and who are the servants? Are public servants really serving us if they monitor us, while no one monitors them?   Shouldn't *they* be monitored to protect the public from abuses of power and money?

A truly safe society would direct cameras and listening devices upon power figures acting as public servants. Upon professionals and politicians who police themselves in areas where the money reaches into Billions or Trillions. A safe society would have a diligent media doing this work, but that seems to no longer be the case.

So spying eyes are on the public, and not on public servants. I wonder if we humans are fooling ourselves, or being perfectly fooled? Either way, cameras always keep watch on the farm animals in the pens, never the farmers. That should be our indicator of just who is being farmed…and who the farmers are.

I dream of an "Accountability Movement", much like movements to help our natural environment. An Accountability Movement could be of help to our social, political and economic environments in the way the Environmental movement is trying to save our natural world. It could help in exposing those who damage the environments that determine our quality of life.

With everything to gain and virtually nothing to lose (except hidden crime and corruption), I am excited to think about an entire new field, open to anyone, designed to reward those brave humans who stand up and speak for the public good.

No qualifications are needed for this industry, and there are no barriers to entry. Just public rewards for those who creatively engage in truth-telling or blowing the whistle on practices which farm humans, or harm the planet or our social systems. It is simply a few billion eyeballs paying attention to the hidden crimes of power and wealth, making the stories public, and being rewarded for doing the right thing. Just imagine incentivizing people and society for doing what is right, instead of rewarding them for doing wrong. More details on this topic can be found in the "solutions" area near the end of the book.

Chapter 37

Rentier Capitalism

<u>This Chapter is about:</u> Systemic tricks to create a "guaranteed income without having to work for it". Farming Humans trick #28.

<u>It is important because:</u> It is the easiest game going, for the "Rentier" who can obtain a rigged advantage.

Have you ever heard the word "Rentier"?
(pronounced "Ront-e-ay" like the French would pronounce it)

Rent-seeking is where an individual seeks to increase their own wealth without creating any benefits or wealth to society. Rent-seekers generally obtain large financial and economic gains at an enormously small cost, often a bribe or change to the law. In the public sector, for example, government lobbyists are hired to sway public policy to benefit their companies and punish their competitors. Rules and laws get changed to benefit the rent-seeker **only** and none other. This is called rent seeking.

"Rentier Capitalism" is an unequal, unfair manipulation of society where rules, laws or legislation are altered in a manner to produce an economic benefit for certain parties over others. It extracts value from society.

"Rent seeking" is not to be confused with owning a two bedroom apartment that someone pays you to live in. That is a simple _property rental_ transaction, where one party provides a space to live and the other provides rent to occupy that space. A fair exchange of value for value.

It is common practice today, to put in place regulations and laws which give special privileges to some over others. If a corporation can rig rules or laws, or obtain the right to print money, or the privilege to self-regulate, they can profit without having to contribute any work beyond rigging the law. This is how the "rentier" gains an advantage over others, by getting his own unfair advantage placed into law.

One demonstration in this book is the creation of the Federal Reserve, granting exclusive money creation rights to a small group of bankers who then profit from this franchise forever. Another was when corporations where declared to be "persons" just so they could save millions in taxes, while keeping all the unique advantages of not being...real persons.

Rentier Capitalism is a form of parasitic behavior that I also call Lawless Capitalism, or capitalism in violation of, or without regard for the public interest. When I began writing this chapter on Renter's vs Rentier's, I observed principles of Rentier Capitalism in nearly every other chapter in the book. It plays a large part in the economic abuse of countless humans. It is the game that some lazy billionaires play. Simply bribe someone to rig the law in your favor, and you have created a guaranteed basic income, without ever having to work for it. It is the perfect crime.

Picture if you can, the indigenous people of North America, Australia, or anywhere else. They lived in a society which believed that the land belonged to all and to no one specifically. It was like the "commons" in previous times. Then came the white man with his self-created rules about ownership and paper documents to claim ownership of land. To natives there was simply no such thing as "ownership" of earth. This was a convoluted idea where ownership of a "derivative", a piece of paper, was considered to equal ownership of earth and water. A belief "construct" created just for those who would benefit.

Nothing could be stranger (or more unfair) to the original inhabitants of the land. They have suffered and lost for hundreds of years by an inability to comprehend or to contend with strange new belief system. It did not have to be a fair system of belief, or even one that respected the original inhabitants of the land. It just had to be created by clever man and enforced by violence.

What goes around comes around, and now all humans, no matter the skin color, are feeling some of that same unfairness in the form of corporate domination. If the meaning of that does not seem clear by now, then I will try to be clearer: "Farming Humans", is not just a story about what is happening to others, it is a story about what is happening to 99% of humans, regardless of color or race. Just like the original inhabitants, nothing could be stranger or more incomprehensible to many people today, than the many clever ways they are being tricked. At least thirty ways to farm humans are listed in this book, and it is by no means a complete list. Not only are they tricks, but to the average member of the public, they are also kept secret. Most people will never even know of their being cheated out of a fair chance on this planet.

The King of England was a "rent-seeker" when he put laws in place requiring American Colonies to purchase tea only from the East Indian Company. The King owned shares in that company so he demanded American Colonies to buy none other. Americans did not like having to pay higher prices and wanted their own free choice in the matter. And they got it.

The East India Company had also been granted competitive advantages over colonial American tea importers to sell tea from its colonies in Asia in American colonies. This led to the Boston Tea Party in which protesters boarded British ships and threw the tea overboard. When protesters successfully prevented the unloading of tea in three other colonies and in Boston, Governor Thomas Hutchinson of the Province of Massachusetts Bay refused to allow the tea to be returned to Britain. This was one of the incidents which led to the American revolution and independence of the American colonies.
Wikipedia

The rent-seeking society puts rigged-rules on billions of people. Unfairly rigged rules are like shackles and chains on some humans but not on others, and cause extreme stress on our societies, on mental and physical health, as well as the health of the planet.

The shackles and chains are belief systems, rules, regulations and laws which the rent-seeker creates or invents so that the outcome is beneficial to themselves, without regard, and without fairness to the rest of society. It is the systematic tilting of the playing field in their favor, which puts them in a position to profit without doing much beyond simply rigging the rules. That is not capitalism, it is more like self-serving criminality. Organized criminality when considering how many professionals, regulators and legislators are involved.

In many cases, it is a game played by business lawyers and politicians who say, "I have an idea,....lets pretend...." and with a few winks and nods, they have created their unfair advantage. It is The Secret Welfare System for billionaires, or the #AMIP (Assured Maximum Income Program) for billionaires, while the rest get get a social system resembling the cruel, cut-throat aspects of Capitalism.

A fair society would take away the unfair advantages of the rich and the influential. The public is allowed to ask, *"if the system is not fair or equal for all, as prescribed in the founding documents of great nations, then are those systems even legitimate?"* What compels a free nation to follow unfair, illegitimate, or criminally rigged systems? This is partially how 8 billionaires have amassed half of the world's wealth.

Perhaps artificial persons (corporations) and the owners of artificial persons, should lose their unfair advantages. After all, they are nothing but belief systems put in place to give special favor to a few men, sometimes at the expense of all other life on earth.

What a gift that might be to humanity, society and to the planet. I could be wrong, but that is one perspective that I am grateful to be able to share.

Another example of "rentier" is seen in the entitled access to justice systems and the law that is given to lawyers, and the sometimes disrespect for ordinary people who try to access that very same justice system without a lawyer. That could be an example of the "monopolization" where certain people obtain control of the justice system. This monopoly makes earning their income easier since the demand for lawyers is increased. Lawyers make more money by having monopoly or near-monopoly access to justice systems, and those who want equal access to justice need to consider hiring a lawyer. This gives economic advantages to the legal industry and disadvantages to the public at large. It makes our society more fragile and again more unfair to some people. Recall the principles of democracy being "…*all eligible citizens being* *equal before the law* and having equal access to legislative processes."

Even bad lawyers survive in an environment where it is almost a requirement to have a lawyer representing you in the justice system. Imagine if the restaurant industry were to obtain a similar monopoly, where no one could eat without doing so at a restaurant. Even the most horrible of restaurants would survive under such foolishness, and that is how "Rentier Capitalism" works. This is an extreme example, but what if equal access to justice is just as important in a free country?

Another example might be the use of industry protection laws, somewhat like "self"-regulation for the financial industry, or the Federal Reserve Act which gave away the monopoly to create every US dollar. A few rules carefully rigged results in billions or trillions of public money and benefits, flowing in the direction of a dozen men. It creates permanent riches for those already rich men.

The cost to America, of giving to private bankers, an activity which could as easily be done by the country itself, is enough to place the country into permanent debt and ever-growing poverty. The cost is incalculable, but is among the greatest economic sinkholes draining countries today.

In 1996 U.S. President Bill Clinton signed The Telecommunications Act of 1996. The legislation's primary goal was deregulation of the converging broadcasting and telecommunications markets.

The stated objective was to open up markets to competition by removing barriers to entry. Instead, it reduced the number of major media companies from around 50 in 1983 to 10 in 1996 and 6 in 2005. (Wikipedia)

Consumer activist Ralph Nader argued that the Act was an example of corporate welfare spawned by political corruption. "Corruption is the abuse of entrusted power for private gain."   Transparency International.

(revisit page 95 for a second example of Bill Clinton selling out America to the highest bidder)

> Breach of trust by public officer
> 122 Every official who, in connection with the duties of their office, commits fraud or a breach of trust, whether or not the fraud or breach of trust would be an offense if it were committed in relation to a private person, is guilty of
>   (a) an indictable offense and liable to imprisonment for a term of not more than five years; or
>   (b) an offense punishable on summary conviction.
> https://laws-lois.justice.gc.ca/eng/acts/c-46/section-122.html

Rentier Capitalism allows the wealthy or powerful to acquire wealth at a much faster rate than other members in society, by rigging the playing field against all other players.

Rent Seeking tips the playing field from level, to one where the advantages are tilted in favor of the Rentier, while the rest must play in an unfair game. In business this makes money rain down into the hands of those who obtained the rigged advantage.

Chapter 38
Human Effects of Systemic Unfairness

This Chapter is about: How humans are physically and mentally harmed, when systems are allowed to become unfairly rigged.

It is important because: It is self-evident simply watching the daily news in any modern society. Even if you are doing OK in a rigged society, will your children and grandchildren fare as well as you?

Trysh Travis, author of "The Language of the Heart: A Cultural History of the Recovery Movement from Alcoholics Anonymous to Oprah Winfrey"

"Substance abuse can't really be addressed without an address of the context in which the abuse occurs....that means attention to poverty, lack of meaningful well-paying work, and persistent structural racism and inequality."

"Not at all drug users use drugs because of racism, not all drug users use drugs because they can't get jobs, but *there are strong correlations between substance use and systemic inequality.*"

"Those factors are really unpleasant to think about as well as hard to address... and I think that the unpleasantness means that people just don't really want to address them."

"Until people are willing to reckon with the fact that these things (systemic inequalities) are man-made, they are human-made, they are cultural, they are social, they are political and economic."

"Until people are willing to reckon with that aspect of what 'structures' (causes) substance use and abuse, I don't see any real progress being made anytime soon."
1:00:00 to 1:05:00
From host Geoff Turner, host of CBC's ON DRUGS. Rehab, recovery and the history of 12-step thinking
http://www.cbc.ca/radio/ondrugs/rehab-recovery-and-the-history-of-12-step-thinking-1.4623343

Is the person in the image below suffering from laziness, hopelessness, or unfairness? How do you know, or do you simply make a judgement? Could you imagine one of your family members in this position if they were treated to the system inequality that any first-world country allows? What makes you think that your own children will be immune?

Will your children's children inherit a free and fair world, or one rigged against them?

Are governments mere corporate-servants now, instead of public servants? Do governments secretly serve other influencers under the table? Isn't that a use of public power for private gain?

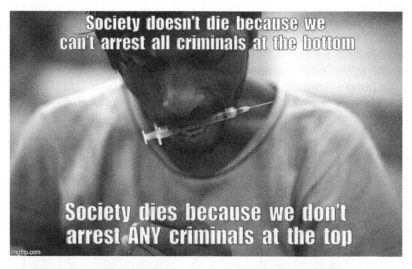

I believe that by ignoring almost 100% of crimes done by our "trusted" criminals, the result is that the most vulnerable of our society is forced into acts of hopeless desperation.

Larry Elford 2 min trailer, Secret Systemic Financial "Dis-Ease"
https://www.youtube.com/watch?v=_Q9zHF9Yb2g

The full presentation is 30 minutes and located here:
https://www.youtube.com/watch?v=-MzQhVt_fc0

Chapter 39

Banking

<u>This Chapter is about:</u>   Politicians, regulators and government agencies who pretend to serve the public, while serving another master.
<u>It is important because:</u>   It causes fragile societies which are subject to black swan events, including systemic failure or breakdown.

Politicians who sell out the public interest to the highest bidders are committing rent-seeking crimes. These are crimes which every member of the public must pay for, while only the criminals get rich.

In the image below from 1999, those rent seekers would go on to gamble *their banks, and your country,* to the point of nearly collapsing the entire financial system (2008). They would then receive government rewards (bailouts and bonus's) for their gambling schemes. They would repeat the trick again around 2020.

THE BANKING ACT OF 1933

Also known as Glass-Steagall, the Banking Act of 1933 effectively separated risky speculative investment banking from traditional, FDIC protected functions like issuing mortgages and small business loans. The repeal of this law by Bill Clinton in 1999 led directly to the toxic mortgage-fueled meltdown of 2008... the root cause of our current economic situation.

Even the FCAC, the Financial Consumer Agency of Canada is in the game. FCAC was caught letting Canadian banks review and redact reports on Parliamentary hearings into bank abuses, *prior to* releasing the findings to the public. See image of blacked out documents below obtained by CBC news.

Is a government which will do this to the public even a legitimate government any longer? It seems like a dual injury of taxation *plus* criminal-representation?

It turns out that the FCAC, which appears for all intents and purposes to be a government organization, acting in the public interests, is in truth an industry funded entity, paid, connected and influenced by the industry they claim to police.

The public is told they are safe and protected from financial abuses, and it is actually the financially industry which is carefully protected and insulated...from public accountability.

FCAC
sent the big banks a draft copy of its report on aggressive sales tactics, they replied — every page was blacked out in the documents obtained under Access to Information laws. (CBC).

More than half the pages of a draft of the report obtained via Access to Information had words or entire sections redacted. (Andrew Lee/CBC)
Erica Johnson
Senior Investigative Reporter CBC News: Go Public

There is very little effort to truly protect the public. Virtually all effort in Canada is done by agencies and regulatory bodies whom are paid, stacked, or otherwise influenced by the financial industry. Most protection is mere facade. I now realize that it has probably been rigged this way long before many of us were born. Rigged regulatory systems are another example of "rent seeking".

It is simple corruption.

2008 crisis and banker bailout story

With financial markets deregulated and allowed back to their gambling-addictions, new derivative investments were being packaged with inflated, unrated sub-prime mortgages. Because they were pre-destined to crash, it provided the perfect setup to profit at the expense of cheating the public out of billions. It was a turning point in the 21st Century for the public to see that something was very unfair with the system.

"Self" regulating banks and investment dealers packaged up junk mortgage-backed investments and dumped them on an unsuspecting public. The crash nearly brought the world economy to a halt, causing government to step in, and save the very people who caused the collapse.

Imagine an explosion at a nuclear reactor, where the explosion was caused deliberately, and where the "fallout" was bailout money rather than radioactive fallout. The fallout did not affect the planet equally or fairly, but rained money upon the very people… who caused the disaster to occur…while the costs, pain and suffering fell upon the public.

Turn back to page 198 and check the image of the "professionals" who set up this perfect crime upon society. See the smiles on their faces. The smiles of successful Rentiers…

The Emergency Economic Stabilization Act of 2008, often called the "bank bailout of 2008," was proposed by Treasury Secretary Henry Paulson, passed by the 110th United States Congress, and signed into law by President George W. … Estimates for the total cost of the bailout to the government are as much as $29 trillion.

Wikipedia

Lets see if we can break this Rentier case down just a bit.

1. Hank Paulson is a former Chairman of Goldman Sachs.

2. Goldman Sachs was one of the companies to gamble enough money to risk the collapse of the banking system, the US economy and perhaps the global economy. (2008 etc)

3. Goldman Sachs formerly was an investment company, which would not have made it likely to be bailed out in case of trouble.

4. However, it converted itself into a global bank holding company, Goldman Sachs Group, and thus became part of the list of essential banks which were to be bailed out using taxpayer funds. (Rentier Win!)

4. Hank Paulsen presided over an investment company that gambled and lost enough money to need government rescue, and then Hank Paulsen moved from Goldman to become head of the US Treasury under President George W Bush...to give his former company a multi-billion dollar bailout. (Rentier Payoff!)

5. Every American must absorb the cost to bail out the Rentiers, since every bailout is debt added upon the taxpayer.

6. It is a crime to manipulate public government money or authority to benefit private or special interests...except in a corrupt system.

Henry Merritt "Hank" Paulson Jr. is an American banker who served as the 74th Secretary of the Treasury. Prior to his role in the Department of the Treasury, Paulson was the chairman and chief executive officer of Goldman Sachs. Wikipedia

---

Chinese saying:
法不责众-
"The law cannot be enforced when everyone is an offender"

Chapter 40
Organized Crime

<u>This Chapter is about:</u> The fiduciary-duty of a professional "adviser" vs the suitability-standard ("good enough") of the broker/sales "advisor". Farming Humans trick #29.

<u>It is important because:</u> "Suitability" is the standard of the Dollar Store product, and about one million so-called investment professionals are selling products using just that standard in North America. Your future life savings may depend on learning to spot the Dollar Store financial "Advisor".

What if investing your life savings involved a confidence game, where you were the only person involved who was not in on the game? What if this were the case for 100 million North American investors? You think someone in authority would have told you about this trick by now.

What if the difference between a state or SEC registered investment "adviser", and the "adviser-like facsimile" known as an "advisor" was intentionally concealed from 99.9% of retail investors in North America? I assure you that 99.9% of investors do not yet know the difference. The deception is that well orchestrated.

What if the difference between the best quality investments recommended by registered fiduciary advisers, and the expensive packaged "investment-like products" pushed for commissions by salespersons, was enough to cut your retirement savings capital by more than half, over a lifetime of investing?

Is it fair to millions of North American investors to be duped and deceived by misrepresentation of a professional registration category? This is something ordinarily called fraud, when a doctor, lawyer or dentist is caught doing this. Yet the financial industry get a free pass from fraud.

The effects of running this confidence game today is a financial harvest of the public of epic proportions. My calculations in Canada estimate a greater harvest of the public by fraudulent misrepresentation than the financial cost of all measured crimes in the land. We are talking real financial security taken from the public.

Now imagine that the regulators of the financial services industry were hand picked and hand-paid by the financial services industry itself? What if one could earn $700,000 or more as one of those regulators?

I hope that readers will begin a new investment journey, one that will take them a bit closer to knowing what kind of financial "guide" or "advisor" they truly have. My hope is that you will begin with a few simple steps in order to find out what game you are participating in:

1. Learn _for yourself_ the difference between a "fiduciary" duty of care to an investor, verses the "suitability standard" of care used in commission selling of investment products. Never take verbal assurances from an investment sales agent. It may mean the difference between getting good investments, or "investment-like" products from "adviser-like" people.

2. Obtain written confirmation of a fiduciary obligation, on company letterhead, before accepting verbal promises from any investment seller. This is the _critical point of failure_ for every retail investor. They always "trust their guy".

3. If you cannot obtain clear, written proof of a fiduciary duty of care, then you are at risk of being provided with "investment-like products", sold by "adviser-like" people. Products designed to unjustly enrich the seller and the dealer, at the expense of underperformance for the investor. It's your life savings…

4. My first book was about all of the above, and more, and it is called "ABOUT YOUR FINANCIAL MURDER…" It can be ordered online at LuLu.com.

Putting aside the unique risks of the investment industry for a moment, let's consider the bigger picture of organized professional crime and it's impact on society.

What is the difference between "crime" and "professional crime"? One is usually easy to spot, and the other is concealed behind well dressed persons living in nice homes, driving nice vehicles to nice offices. Persons in your church, on your school board and yes, members of your police commission. Many seek out congratulations in the newspaper for their charitable efforts and contributions to society.

Former RCMP Money Laundering expert Bill Majcher tells of his experience and frustration of trying to investigate the activities of lawyers, and how much of a blockage to doing his job this profession can put before the police. It is worth a listen to better understand how professions can "circle the wagons" around themselves in a way to keep the law out.

His interview begins at 1:05:00 on the YouTube video titled "France is Lost, The Fix is In: Gerald Celente & RCMP Inspector Bill Majcher".

They also have another "easy out", namely to simply point to the professional self-regulating body involved and say "let them handle it". It lets overworked police go on with their work, and allows professionals to police themselves.

Some professions then become elevated a half-step above the average man on the street. They get to police themselves when others are not so lucky. Then there are professionals who operate through a corporation which may give them the benefits of "self" regulation and further benefits of corporate immunity. Twice elevated above the man on the street. Two superior powers, based on a simple game of "lets pretend…."

Having this superior status or elevated protection gives professional crime the ability to flourish in secrecy. If some can spread tax evasion or money laundering "work" across a few borders, they can operate in even greater freedom from being caught.

Gangs sometimes win. Professional gangs <u>always</u> seem to win. Why?
Organized professional gangs are an entity that survives from generation to generation, in a similar way that a profession and a corporation can exist forever and easily morph its shape and its public perception over time. Corporations and professions, never die. They just get better at making hidden underground connections and quid pro quo's, like a grove of Aspen trees.

Agnotology 101 Pop Quiz

What if true Puppet Masters do not "run **for**…the office of presidents?"
What if the true Puppet Masters "**run** the offices of presidents?"

Is that the secret to organized professional crime? Stay in control by staying invisible, and in the background, never seeking the spotlight, yet manipulating the controls like the Wizard of Oz?

In 1815, Rothschild made his famous statement: "I care not what puppet is placed upon the throne of England to rule the Empire on which the sun never sets. The man who controls the British money supply controls the British Empire, and I control the British money supply."

Nathan Mayer Rothschild - Wikipedia

Perhaps the best indicator, the "tell", if you will of this great con is that the person who is trying desperately to keep your attention looking "over here…then over there", is not the master, not the professional. The attention seeker, the vote seeker, is perhaps nothing but the dancing, singing clown. The distraction. The public falls for the singing, dancing clown (or the war or whatever) every time.

For a stark illustration of how that looks, watch just a few minutes (on YouTube) of "Watch Donald Trump Take Down WWE's Vince McMahon Back in 2007". It's a good example of what the dancing clown show looks like. Remember, this man became President of a country less than ten years after this performance.
https://www.youtube.com/watch?v=jkghtyxZ6rc&t=5s

Chapter 41

Politicians as "Double Agents"

This Chapter is about: Political or public service chameleons as bait and switch artists? A continuation of Farming Humans Trick #30.

It is important because: A free and prosperous society depends upon keeping crooks out of government...just like keeping the hogs out of the creek if you want clean water.

If financial advisors can act as "double-agents", what do we call politicians, who pretend to serve the public while serving other private and corporate masters? Treasonous?

How does society stand a chance, when politicians promise to serve the public interest, and then fold like a cheap tent to serve billionaires, bankers, and corporations?

Some politicians only stay in power if they have enough money to keep getting re-elected, and they can only gain the money to be re-elected if they take money from private interests. Thanks to Citizens United (2010) in the U.S., money is now deemed to be "speech" (another man-made belief), and corporate money floods into political campaigns as donations. Politicians are then in either a "quid pro quo" obligation, or a "double bind", to deliver something in return to those donors, or they risk not getting those cheques again.

The person who owns a corporation, can use the corporation to bribe, influence, buy or corrupt the political class into rigging rules and laws against everyone else in the nation. The end result is a damaged society, a wounded nation, and transfer of wealth to politicians, so that they sell out the interests of millions of people, to benefit the interests of a few. Democracy seems broken when this happens.

Chapter 42

MILITARY might...

<u>This Chapter is about:</u> How the ultimate power can be a useful tool for those seeking to monopolize the world's wealth.

<u>It is important because:</u> What if global bankers are using your military as their enforcers and "repo men"? "Pay up or we are coming in..."

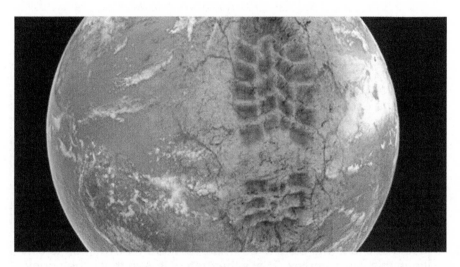

"Terrorism is one of the only areas where white people do most of the work, yet take none of the credit." Ken Cheng·

What if some of what the media calls "terrorism" is more like a retaliation penalty in a hockey game?

If you are in the game, and the referee is looking the other way, an opponent might crack you over the head with his stick, yet there is generally no penalty if the hit is not spotted by the referee.

Then, when you realize what happened, you may lose your cool and rush to retaliate against the person that attacked you. The referee is often watching when the angry rush to retaliate occurs, and this earns you a penalty. That retaliation penalty is a bit like some things that get labeled as terrorism. It may not be the root cause, but the effect, the result, or an emotional reaction to an original offense. We only label it terrorism when it is done by "other people", while we ignore any cause, fault or original attack when it is done by "our people". Similar to how we lose our mind when someone cuts us off in traffic, because it is done by someone else, but we rationalize and excuse ourselves when we cut someone else off…right?

Let just one person "act out", in retaliation against what may be murder or genocide in another narrative, and we lose our mind. We truly should not be losing our mind unless we are certain that we did not do the original harm, or create the first offense.

Retired U.S. Army Colonel Lawrence Wilkerson, who served as Secretary of State Colin Powell's chief of staff from 2002 to 2005, says the escalation of tensions between the U.S. and Iran today is a continuation of two decades of U.S. policy disasters in the Middle East, starting with the 2003 run-up to war with Iraq under the Bush administration.

"America exists today to make war. How else do we interpret 19 straight years of war and no end in sight? It's part of who we are.

It's part of what the American Empire is," says Wilkerson. "We are going to cheat and steal to do whatever it is we have to do to continue this war complex. That's the truth of it. And that's the agony of it."

https://www.democracynow.org/2020/1/13/lawrence_wilkerson-_american_empire_war?fbclid=IwAR1CINv6LmGZ3T9Eo-D8fj_rd5miF8RyiH78Un8kCy7LEdDLFGC2lB3E71R4

I am in not condoning violence of any kind, I am suggesting that the game of farming humans includes lawless acts, by our own governments and institutions, designed to do serious harm to others, in order to use that harm for political or economic purposes.

Again, search "All wars are bankers wars", on YouTube.

"U.S. HAS SPENT SIX TRILLION DOLLARS ON WARS THAT KILLED HALF A MILLION PEOPLE SINCE 9/11", NEWSWEEK REPORT SAYS

Brown University's Watson Institute for International and Public Affairs published its annual "Costs of War" report Wednesday, taking into consideration the Pentagon's spending and its Overseas Contingency Operations account, as well as "war-related spending by the Department of State, past and obligated spending for war veterans' care, interest on the debt incurred to pay for the wars, and the prevention of and response to terrorism by the Department of Homeland Security."

The final count revealed, "The United States has appropriated and is obligated to spend an estimated $5.9 trillion (in current dollars) on the war on terror through Fiscal Year 2019, including direct war and war-related spending and obligations for future spending on post 9/11 war veterans."

"In sum, high costs in war and war-related spending pose a national security concern because they are unsustainable," the report concluded. "The public would be better served by increased transparency and by the development of a comprehensive strategy to end the wars and deal with other urgent national security priorities."

https://www.newsweek.com/us-spent-six-trillion-wars-killed-half-million-1215588?fbclid=IwAR1RsxKn7XxRmOPrF7mmARhfp0y

Chapter 43

Media as Handmaids and Spin Doctors

This Chapter is about: How mainstream media is now a fully owned subsidiary of the Corporate machine. Farming Humans Trick #32.

It is important because: If you are getting your news from a network, you are not always getting "news"…you are getting commercial "messaging". (Otherwise known as propaganda.)

Watching the amount of distraction and mis-information in the news today is like being shown images of Disneyland, and being told that it is a true functioning city.

A *claim* about something is not the same as a *fact* about something. We've lost this in our media, sometime around the 1971-era when the US had to default on its last gold standard. Many things seem to have changed after that default.

North American media seems to have become a financially captured handmaid, profiting handsomely by walking in lockstep with what corporate control would like the public to believe.

Recall that in a winner-take-all world where the world's reserve currency can be printed for nearly free, the printers make a dividend on each dollar created as part of their franchise arrangement, and then they can lend those dollars at further interest. With that kind of power they can own, make or break any sector of the economy they choose.

A captured media is a vital component in professional organized crime. They help to spread confusion and disinformation to an extent that would make Russian spies of the 1980's proud.

Disinformation is false information spread deliberately to deceive. This is a subset of misinformation, which also may be unintentional.
The English word disinformation is a loose translation of the Russian dezinformatsiya,[derived from the title of a KGB black propaganda department. Joseph Stalin coined the term, giving it a French-sounding name to claim it had a Western origin. Russian use began with a "special disinformation office" in 1923.[Disinformation was defined in Great Soviet Encyclopedia (1952) as "false information with the intention to deceive public opinion". Wikipedia

Putin was in the KGB during the era when KGB agents were expected to contribute disinformation as part of their job. And you say that now disinformation is his favorite tool. Why do you think it's his favorite tool?

ELLICK: "Well, disinformation has a lot of advantages. First of all, it's very cheap. It's certainly more affordable than tanks and aerial bombardments. It's also a long game. So the fruits of disinformation pay off over many, many years. And Putin is not - unlike many politicians in the West, Putin doesn't have a four- or eight-year term. He's been in power for a really long time, and there appears to be no end in sight of his rule. And disinformation definitely requires a long view. There's a great quote in one of these videos that surfaced from the 1980s. And someone said that it's like when water hits a rock in the middle of a rainforest, you return a few years later and the water is still hitting the rock, but there's no dent in the rock. And then you return 10 years later, and there's a small dent in the rock. And you return 20 years later, and there's a massive hole in the rock. And that's sort of how a disinformation campaign succeeds, with a really, really long view."

https://www.npr.org/2018/11/15/668209008/inside-the-russian-disinformation-playbook-exploit-tension-sow-chaos

What is going on now in the west (and elsewhere) is a farce, a circus and a distraction. Like my cowboy friend Will used to say, "any fool knows that if you intend to rob the town bank, first you set fire to the stables…" Mainstream media today is in charge of setting the stable fires.

Chapter 44

Privately Owned Central Banking
(Winner in the "rent seeking" category)

<u>This Chapter is about:</u> How to pocket the biggest portion of the wealth of a nation, or the entire world. (I still believe this to be the root cause, or the greatest trick in the world for Farming Humans)

<u>It is important because:</u> It appears to be a foundational element of farming humanity.

We talked about "Rentier" or "rent seeking" in Chapter 37.

Earning a "guaranteed minimum income", without having to work for it is the intended result for anyone who rigs the system like a Rentier.

Corporations who influence politicians and get legislation favoring their business have often gained a "guaranteed minimum income, without having to work for it."

The financial advisor who confuses, and spins investment customers, using false-titles and false-trust, gives themselves a "guaranteed minimum income, without having to work for it…"

The politician who sells out the public, for campaign contributions from a special interest group give themselves a "guaranteed minimum income, without having to work for it…"

It is all about finding ways to cheat and to find shortcuts.

If government grants a "Monopoly" to create a nation's money out of thin air, to a private group, and give that group priority access to where the money gets deposited (their own banks) then that private group has effectively captured the biggest portion of the wealth of a nation. Just look at the private banks who own the Fed and judge for yourself. They have obtained a "basic guaranteed minimum income, without having to work for it"…for over 100 years now.

The U.S., and Canadian society etc., would gain Trillions from a fair system of currency or money creation owned by the public, and not by private interests. Bankers might not benefit as much, but the country would be ahead by trillions. With the money being "handled" by private interests, and society taxed to fund those private interests, society begins to look a bit like it is being farmed.

The amount of money on the Federal Reserve balance sheet (debt owed by the nation) was around One Trillion before the mortgage bubble collapse at the end of 2007.

Today, after bailing out the banks and billionaires who gambled themselves into the ground, the amount of debt (owed by the American public) is touching $7 Trillion.

That means the country added seven times more debt to bail out Billionaires and banks from their gambling addiction, and those same billionaire gamblers were many of the banks who own the Fed…who bailed out the gamblers, who own the Fed, who earn a dividend from every dollar created….and so on…I lose track after a while of just how many times a Federal Reserve banker can get paid on a single US dollar.

Another way to look at it is that the Fed created seven times as much money, as was created in the first 200 years of the country, just to bail out the banks…and they put the debt on the backs of all the working taxpayers in the land.

To put a sharper point on it, if I am a billionaire getting bailed out, I get billions in cash TODAY, and every taxpayer gets to pay for it, forever more. The banks who own the Fed are giving themselves yet another Trillion-dollar bailout, and once again putting most of the cost on the backs of US taxpayers.

This comes close to shining a light into the daylight robbery that the Federal Reserve has done to the United States for over 100 years.

Smart people usually ask, "why doesn't the government just issue and print it's own money, using a government-owned Central Bank instead of a private one?" The government issues IOU's, notes, bills, etc, to back up the currency. Why doesn't the US Treasury simply issue currency notes (money) just as easily as they issue the IOU's, and skip the middleman? The politicians of the day (and today) were duped and/or corrupted seems why.

Canada is no stand up government in this area either. In 1974, around the time that Nixon was defaulting on the gold standard of the US Dollar, Canada was being told (by international bankers) that the Bank of Canada was no longer allowed to fund our giant infrastructure projects itself, and that it now had to borrow the money from private bankers instead.
Canada COMERS story of the removal of power from the Bank of Canada
Rocco Galati - Debt Owed to Foreign Bankers and Bank of Canada Lawsuit

https://www.youtube.com/watch?v=LUwUKPucYlM&feature=share

Readers can view the Federal Reserve balance sheet at

https://www.federalreserve.gov/monetarypolicy/bst_recenttrends.htm

Chapter 45

2020 Negative Interest Rates

<u>This Chapter is about:</u> Trying to better understand Billionaire Games and…Hunger Games.

<u>It is important because:</u> Our world is based on money, which is man-made, and man-made systems of belief have an ability to rule or ruin society.

Has the "time value" of money become irrelevant?

It was 1971, when Nixon took the U.S. off the gold standard, meaning that the US dollar was no longer backed by, or convertible into gold. You can argue all day about whether gold is of any value, or should or should not be used to "back" a currency, but lets avoid that argument for a moment in case there are bigger questions involved.

The time value of money (TVM) is the concept that money today, is worth more than the identical sum of money in the future. In simple terms it means that a person would prefer to have $100 today, than to receive $100 one year from today. To cause a person to "delay the gratification" of having $100 today, they would want to be promised a greater amount than $100, to induce them to delay. This is the *time value of money*, which is quoted or calculated as the interest rate. The interest rate is the cost of money.

Interest rates put a value upon that one year delay, to adjust so that someone who was willing to wait (delayed gratification) one year to be paid, would be compensated for waiting. They may demand to be paid $110 one year from now, in return for lending $100 today. That would mean a 10% rate of interest is charged.

The US removed all limits on money creation in 1971, when Nixon removed (defaulted on?) the convertibility of US Dollars into gold. Yet since money is used to represent and to purchase limited assets of value, like land, resources, and goods, there could come a time when there are *not enough real assets of value* for all the less-real pieces of paper.

When an ever increasing amount of money, is used to represent the wealth of a finite planet, the money becomes "worth less" over time. At near-infinite levels of money creation, the currency can become literally "worthless". Google "Weimar Republic Death of Money" to see this in history. Or Zimbabwe, Yugoslavia, Hungary, Venezuela etc.

Thought Experiment…

Money created out of nothing, causes "infinite prosperity" for a few people on a planet of eight billion. A few thousand men get to become Billionaires, while billions of people are left out of the game. This is due to a repeal of the laws of poverty for a few thousand "special" people, and brutal application of the laws of poverty upon the rest. We have literally created two (or more) different games in one society, the Free-Money Game for Billionaires at one extreme, and the Hunger Games for persons who must live in debt (or on the street) at the other.

These two distinct socio-economic systems exist today in first-world countries, even the one where "All men are created equal." One system is sometimes labeled "socialism", or the welfare state, and that is the state that corporations and some billionaires have <u>gained for their own personal benefit</u>. In this system, people are forgiven their debts and mistakes, and treated with all the generosity that the state can hand out. These people live on constant infusions of public (taxpayer) money, and they own yachts and jets to get to their private islands. We call these people "winners", and the media worships them like Gods. The other social-state offers the harsh realities of capitalism and it lets only the "strong" survive while the weak are given no help. The weaker people can be seen living beneath tarps or bridges in any developed country and we call those people "lazy". There may be little analysis or accuracy of either "label", as humans (speaking for myself) tend to believe either (a) what the media tells them, or (b) what best suits their instincts or their internal self-serving narrative.

CEO Of Wall Street Bank That Took $25 Billion Bailout Warns Of Socialism For Everyone Else

$25 Billion of public money for this guy's bank (above)…and yet we hear complaints about a basic income for our most vulnerable people "will make them lazy"! "Winner takes all" is the mantra of the financial sociopath.

I wonder if we can see NEGATIVE INTEREST RATES more clearly if we view them like the delayed gratification found in the Children's Marshmallow Experiments?

Who has not heard of the classroom experiments where each child is given some sugary, tasty marshmallows, with a choice attached?

The choice offered to the children go something like this:

"Before we begin I am going to give each student two delicious sugary marshmallows. You may chose to eat your marshmallows right away, and you are welcome to do so, or, …you can choose to wait ten minutes without eating your marshmallows, and we will then give you two more. Those who eat their marshmallows right away will have two marshmallows to eat, and those who wait ten minutes will get to eat four marshmallows."

"You are allowed to do whatever you choose. The ten minutes time begins now."

The Stanford marshmallow experiment was a study on delayed gratification in 1972 led by psychologist Walter Mischel, a professor at Stanford University. In this study, a child was offered a choice between one small but immediate reward, or two small rewards if they waited for a period of time. During this time, the researcher left the room for about 15 minutes and then returned. The reward was either a marshmallow or pretzel stick, depending on the child's preference. In follow-up studies, the researchers found that children who were able to wait longer for the preferred rewards tended to have better life outcomes, as measured by SAT scores educational attainment, body mass index, and other life measures. A replication attempt with a more diverse sample population, over 10 times larger than the original study, showed only half the effect of the original study. The replication suggested that economic background, rather than willpower, explained the other half.

Wikipedia

The observations are supposed to teach "delayed gratification", "impulse control", decision making and consequences. I like the experiment and I presume a man like Warren Buffet would approve as well, since it can be seen as a comparison to the time value of money, or to the compound growth effect of money over time. Warren is arguably the world's top human at understanding delayed financial gratification. If you have not read his biography SNOWBALL, I recommend it for anyone wanting a good story as well as a glimpse into one of the world's great financial minds.

Whether marshmallows or money, humans prefer to have their reward now, instead of waiting, and it is only through offering an additional quantity ("added interest") that will encourage the wise and the patient to delay our human instincts for instant gratification.

Negative interest rates, (which some countries now have) violates the "time value of money" principle of delayed gratification. Now lets imagine the same child's marshmallow experiment where the instructions reflect the opposite of normal principles of time, delay and reward.

"Those students who choose to eat their two marshmallows immediately, can do so, but those who choose to wait the ten minutes will have only one marshmallow to eat. To be clear, if you eat your marshmallows now, you get two marshmallows, and if you wait you only get one."

What do you think the children decide to do? What would you do? Would you prefer to eat two marshmallows now, or wait for ten minutes and get one? That is how negative interest rates act.

How did we get to where negative interest rates are even possible? It seems almost like repealing the law of gravity. Of course natural laws like gravity cannot be repealed, but the interesting thing about man made laws, and belief systems is that they <u>can</u> be repealed. Here we get into natural laws of prosperity, and of poverty. We will explain them later, hopefully, but continuing on with the negative interest rate story, *what if printing an exponentially larger number of US dollars (or any currency) could outpace the ability to increase the finite wealth or assets that those dollars are now chasing?*

There would be too much money and not enough assets to spend that money on. Infinite bits of paper money would be chasing after a finite quantity of real assets. (money could become less sought-after than toilet paper during a pandemic...:)

Not only might this produce negative interest rates, due to the supply/demand balance of money, but this might also cause "asset bubbles" where the price of real estate, or any other asset could be pushed higher and higher by those near-infinite dollars. It spells inflation when too much money chases too few goods, and this is where the billionaire class gets to buy real estate, yachts and jets, while the average person can no longer even afford to live in their own neighborhood. This is what repealing the laws of poverty (for a few) looks like, and repealing the laws of prosperity (for the rest).

It results in an unfair and unjust use of a government asset (the right to produce a nation's currency or money) <u>for the sole benefit of one tiny sector of the population</u>. Those most closely connected to the money creation machine, the super-rich and well connected.

It is because of this past 100 years of "private abuse of a public asset", combined with the limited liability that corporations have enjoyed, that I believe that the public (excluding corporations) deserve a "Debt Jubilee", to restart a rigged society. Even that may not restore fairness but it would be a beginning.
See the "Cantillon Effect" coming up in two pages for the unique advantages created for those closest to the money creation machine.

This brings us back to the "Marshmallow Experiment of delayed gratification", but lets now use "world assets" instead of marshmallows. In a world of near infinite money creation, each trillion dollars created, "devalues" the purchasing power of all money in terms of how much shares, real estate, yachts, jets or copper that can be purchased...or looking at the other side, shares, real estate, yachts or jets go up in price as there are more billionaires with more money in their pockets to give for these and other things. This is one reason why the increase in homeless people.

The adult marshmallow question then becomes, do you spend your billions now to buy the new Gulfstream G650 (2014 Price: $65 million), or do you delay buying the item knowing that you will need millions more to buy the same jet next year? (2017 price $72 million)

This is what happens when we stop issuing real money (pretend that "real money" refers to gold backed money, prior to its "unbacking" in 1971) and instead use artificial, abstract money. Without tangible backing or some limitation on money creation, our money becomes just another "derivative" creation.

There are some things that tangibly-backed money has, that paper money cannot match:

1. Tangible money is somehow (even if distantly) related to tangible wealth like assets, airplanes, minerals, land, trees, zinc, oil, gold, silver, whatever. Paper money is unlimited and somewhat imaginary. It is money by "fiat" only. Money because "someone says" it is.

2. Tangible money is limited by it's relation to something real. Fiat money can be related to "pie in the sky". (Never trust promises of pie in the sky)

3. Trust (did I mention trust already?) Tangibly-backed money is money that is less cheatable by even the better cheaters on the planet, because it must be related, connected, or tied to real tangible assets.

4. Tangible money, limited in relation to something real, cannot be abused to lure men into destroying the planet for money. But infinite amounts of intangible money can be used as a lure to harvest every living thing in every ocean in the world. (and every tree, every drop of fresh water, etc..)

5. Watch "The Lorax" with your kids, to see how that looks.

The image below shows the "end game" of converting Earth into bits of colored paper. The image portrays the winner of the game...after having acquired most or all of the bits of paper.

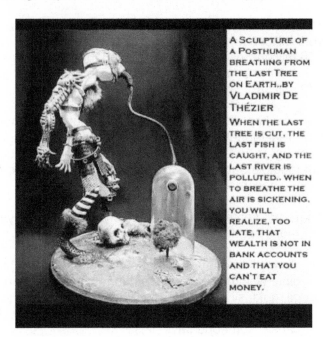

A SCULPTURE OF A POSTHUMAN BREATHING FROM THE LAST TREE ON EARTH..BY VLADIMIR DE THÉZIER

WHEN THE LAST TREE IS CUT, THE LAST FISH IS CAUGHT, AND THE LAST RIVER IS POLLUTED.. WHEN TO BREATHE THE AIR IS SICKENING, YOU WILL REALIZE, TOO LATE, THAT WEALTH IS NOT IN BANK ACCOUNTS AND THAT YOU CAN'T EAT MONEY.

~KC

BANKERS **ALWAYS** COME FIRST

The Cantillon Effect ...continued from Chapter 10
The redistributive effects of money creation were called
Cantillon effects by Mark Blaug after the Franco-Irish economist
Richard Cantillon who experienced the effect of inflation under the
paper money system of John Law at the beginning of the 18th
century.

Cantillon explained that the first to receive newly created money
see their incomes rise whereas the last to receive the newly created money see their purchasing power decline as consumer price
inflation comes about.

With an increase in the stock of money, the cash balances of the
early receivers of the newly created money increase.

The economics of Cantillon effects tells us that financial institutions benefit disproportionately from money creation, since they
can purchase more goods, services, and assets for still relatively
low prices. This conclusion is backed by numerous empirical illus-
trations. For instance, the financial sector contributed massively to
the growth of billionaire's wealth

https://mises.org/library/how-central-banking-increased-inequality

An 18th century French banker and philosopher named Richard
Cantillon noticed an early version of this phenomenon in a book
he wrote called 'An Essay on Economic Theory.' His basic theory
was that who benefits when the state prints a bunch of money is
based on the institutional setup of that state. In the 18th century,
this meant that the closer you were to the king and the wealthy,
the more you benefitted, and the further away you were, the more
you were harmed. Money, in other words, is not neutral. This general observation, that money printing has distributional consequences that operate through the price system, is known as the
"Cantillon Effect".

Using another analogy, imagine a system where we could make it rain any amount on any day chosen, to help a farmer grow his crops. Now imagine being able to "select" which farmers get this gift of rain, and which do not. This is a bit like the benefits of the Cantillion Effect with making it rain…money.

NEGATIVE INTEREST RATES   (continued)

When The Fat Kids on Wall Street consume <u>all</u> of the Marshmallows in the world (and everything else), will there be anything left to consume other than fat Wall Street kids?

Conclusion: In a world of finite resources (a limited number of world marshmallows) and infinite money creation (print all you can dream, and give it <u>first</u> to bankers and billionaires), the billionaire class is like a fat kid who figures out how he can eat every marshmallow in the world with infinitely created money….(While laws of poverty do not apply to fat Wall Street kids, principles of depravity do)

So the decision for Wall Street fat kids is to consume *everything* of value immediately. Own or consume it all, while it is still available, since the supply of anything valuable is finite, and the fat kid's supply of money is infinite, and is losing value every day due to negative interest rates.
If you do not consume it ALL, some other fat Wall Street kid will.

Wall Street's Six Biggest Bailed-Out Banks: Their RAP Sheets & Their Ongoing Crime Spree

What is possible to happen as a result?

Cash becomes trash? I know not, but I suspect as much.

Cash has become an intangible, not a valuable sought after or tangibly grounded asset. It is the "hot potato" that must be passed on to some greater fool. It is a non-income-earning, non-backed, yet global-reserve currency issued by what today resembles a nation in decline.

It could mean we are becoming like the Weimar Republic (read "When Money Dies" The Nightmare Of The Weimar Hyper Inflation) Germany circa 1920

Useless and worthless prediction:

Today (in virtually all Fed market operations and stock markets from 2008 to 2020) we are watching the stables being lit on fire, which is always the perfect old-west distraction, whenever the local bank was to be robbed...or in this case while the entire world is being robbed. The economic disaster that is being "seeded" behind these distractions could be like the Titanic disaster, for entire societies.

Did I mention that this is a useless and worthless prediction, as all predictions of the future are? Consider it my guess if you like.

Quantitative Easing (Blowing Bubbles) by Trillions   (2019)

The Fed knows very well that people are struggling today to keep pace because from December 2007 to July 2010 it secretly pumped a cumulative $29 trillion to bail out Wall Street mega banks and foreign banks. A significant portion of the Fed loans were offered at interest rates below 1 percent when some of these banks were teetering or outright insolvent and couldn't have borrowed in the open market at even 10 percent. Free money.

https://wallstreetonparade.com/2019/10/feds-powell-admits-a-bigger-bailout-for-wall-street-is-coming-feds-balance-sheet-ballooned-by-176-billion-since-september-11/

Publications
WORKING PAPER NO. 698 | December 2011
$29,000,000,000,000: A Detailed Look at the Fed's Bailout by
Funding Facility and Recipient

There have been a number of estimates of the total amount of
funding provided by the Federal Reserve to bail out the financial
system. For example, Bloomberg recently claimed that the cumulative commitment by the Fed (this includes asset purchases plus
lending) was $7.77 trillion. As part of the Ford Foundation project
"A Research and Policy Dialogue Project on Improving Governance of the Government Safety Net in Financial Crisis," Nicola
Matthews and James Felkerson have undertaken an examination
of the data on the Fed's bailout of the financial system—the most
comprehensive investigation of the raw data to date. This working
paper is the first in a series that will report the results of this investigation.

The purpose of this paper is to provide a descriptive account of
the Fed's extraordinary response to the recent financial crisis. It
begins with a brief summary of the methodology, then outlines the
unconventional facilities and programs aimed at stabilizing the existing financial structure. The paper concludes with a summary of
the scope and magnitude of the Fed's crisis response. The bottom
line: a Federal Reserve bailout commitment in excess of $29 tril-
lion.

http://www.levyinstitute.org/publications/29000000000000-a-de-
tailed-look-at-the-feds-bailout-by-funding-facility-and-recipient

Chapter   46

Depressed, Dis-eased, Addicted, Afraid

This Chapter is about: Mental, emotional, physical effects of in-equality which allows the farming of humans. The #1 cause of dis-ability and disease on the planet today.

It is important because: Like the title of my first book, human un-fairness causes pandemics of personal and societal damage.

With stress and anxiety being among the top causes of death and disability today (World Health Organization, (WHO) among others) and "fear of economic uncertainty" as the #1 cause of stress and anxiety…it follows that if there are organized criminal methods by which less fortunate humans are being harmed by rigged games of a few humans, then there is something wrong with those social constructs. Note that I am not saying that all persons should be guaranteed a position in life that is "equal" to other's, but that our systems of justice and governance should not be deliberately rigged by bankers, lawyers and politicians to serve a few humans, while cheating the rest.

Everyone deserves a fair chance in a fair society. (I did not say everyone deserves to be "equal", I said everyone deserves a fair chance)
Selfish acts and abuses of public power rigs and repeals the laws of poverty and prosperity. It is like the US (and many other coun-tries) are right back under the domination of the King of England… remember how that went.

Politicians, corporations, professionals and a number of hand-maids, conspire or collude to become "team players", to "fit in" with the right crowd. Doing so is instinctual and survival related, but not acceptable when done by professionals and public ser-vants and not when this level of tribal behavior causes injustice to millions or billions. That negates the professional or public service status of the act and the actors. It then becomes a Breach of the Public trust or perhaps a criminal RICO file…someday.

To be a team player and to help financially assault millions of people, and cause disability to that country, not to mention poverty, hopelessness, addiction, is not acceptable.

It has become apparent that the addictive traits of the billionaire class, and the power seeking class are not much different from the addictive traits of the hopeless and impoverished class. Similar "hungry ghosts" exist in rich or poor, yet it is still hurts to see the inner pain and addictions of the rich cause so much suffering among the rest.

Addiction support professionals say that things like social exclusion, isolation, trauma and betrayal are some of the core causes of emotional injuries to humans. There are no emotional "pain relievers" better than drugs and alcohol (or perhaps other addictions like jets, yachts, money) for some people.

With rampant and runaway addiction, suicide by addiction and deaths from addiction, it demonstrates that financial lawlessness at the top of many societies is a top cause of disability and death of more vulnerable members of society.

We are killing millions of people and countless other life on the planet in a scramble for a tiny number of people to become billionaires. Making a billion by helping and serving people is a valiant pursuit that we often call "capitalism". However making a billion by rigged or lawless financial predation is crime. It cannot be called capitalism without the word "lawless" in front of it. It can however be seen as addiction…and as organized crime.

Did I mention RICO? (Racketeering
https://www.law.cornell.edu/uscode/text/18/part-I/chapter-96

Did I mention privately filed criminal charges as a right of most citizens?
https://en.wikipedia.org/wiki/Private_prosecution

CHAPTER 47

End "Lawless-Capitalism"
So "Lawful Capitalism" Can Live

This Chapter is about: Justice seems to follow laws of gravity, which means it can easily be applied downwards, but rarely up towards those at the top.

It is important because: We may have to go through some Systemic Crimes Trials, before we get justice.

We have Capitalism without law applied to the richest, the rulers, regulators and the highest ranking in society. This is Free-Money Anarchy (#FMA)...for some

> Anarchy is the state of a society being freely constituted without authorities or a governing body. It may also refer to a society or group of people that totally rejects a set hierarchy. The word anarchy was first used in 1539, meaning "an absence of government". Wikipedia

Cronyism and quid pro quo's now prevent the greatest white collar criminal acts from being held to account. This has led to a "free crime" zone of protection around many of the great crimes against society. The downside of this is that society is being drained of it's financial strength at the same time as its social systems crumble. Those doing the draining are doing just fine.

Our systems of justice do not have the strength or the will to stand against the richest and most powerful. They prefer to stand with them, if given half a chance. This allows a world of free corporate looting and criminality for those in the club, and a frantic "Mad Max" battle of survival for those not in the club.

From the book " The Richest Man Who Ever Lived" by Greg Steinmetz, come lessons and tactics that have helped create the society we live in today. Here are three paragraphs from the book that deserve sharing:

In the wealth of Nations, Adam Smith argued that capitalism provides for all or at least does as much as can be hoped. It succeeds because of what Smith called "The invisible hand."

"An individual looking out for himself is led by an invisible hand to promote an end which was no part his intention," he wrote.

"By pursuing his own interest he frequently promotes that of the society more effectually than when he really intends to promote it."

In other words, individuals out for their own personal gain get rewarded by doing more for the common good and the result is that all parties benefit from a lawful form of capitalism.

The sad reality, is that the lawless pursuit of self interest if left unchecked, leads to crony capitalism, where those in power conspire with rich businessmen to look out for themselves and undermine others. Million-dollar lawyers help the looting. It turns from lawful Capitalism to Rentier Capitalism, which is another term for corruption.

When the "invisible hand" discovers it can exempt, avoid or simply purchase the law, it finds an even easier way of pursuing it's own interests. Adam Smith's argument never considered an age when capitalism could operate outside of rules or laws, or when giant, lawyer-derived creatures could act with impunity, like corporations can. Adam Smith died about 100 years before corporations became "persons", so one wonders how he could have imagined what an "invisible hand" would do when wielded by an "invisible friend"? The Legend of the Ring of Gyges comes to mind.

Capitalism (with laws) is still the better choice of economic systems in my view, in that it brings the greatest rewards to those who do the greatest good for others. Full stop. There is simply something that is fair, magic and hard to argue with in that principle.

Today, however we do not have Capitalism which is supportive of these principles. We have a form of _Lawless Capitalism,_ where the greatest rewards can _more quickly_ go to those who do the greatest harm to society. Certainly, there exist Capitalists who do wonders, creating goods and services within the law, and which benefit society. However one does not have to look very far, to find Billion or Trillion-dollar examples where the riches came at the expense of society, instead of from benefitting humanity. Tobacco, war, dangerous drugs, predatory lending, lobbying, predatory investment advisors, and many others.

The quicker rewards come as a result organized professional lawlessness, which serves those at the top of our economic food chain. Imagine allowing systemic lawlessness which our public servants use…to serve themselves?

In my experience, any crime of a systemic nature, or with dollar-gains approaching $100 million or up, is not likely to gain the attention of career-minded police or prosecutors. That means that billion dollar crimes upon society are not "crimes" in the eyes of police. They are commercial transactions under the control of the regulators, the civil courts, or influential politicians.

Police and government prosecutors seem wise enough, to avoid high value economic crimes, systemic crimes and professional organized crime. They seem to know that going after the richest, the powerful and the connected, is a bad career move. Few, if any, ever go there as a result. Systemic abuses of the public are doubly un-touchable since the rewards of those abuses climb into billions.

Where did US Attorney General Eric Holder go after the mortgage crash of 2008 which nearly collapsed the economy? He did not go after the organized professional gangs responsible, he went back into the service of those gangs, as a wall street lawyer. Quid pro quo is often the choice of the human instinct for self preservation.

This lawless area of capitalism is one of the most important things society must address if it is to survive and thrive. My hopes and imagined solutions near the end of this book may be simplistic, but none easy. But like any simple street addict who is caught in a trap of feeling normal _only_ when doing harm, our society has addictions to power and money which have similarities. The only thing we may have to change…may be everything.

A dreamt-of **"Accountability Movement"** (Chapter 49 in this book) could help expose unchecked power held by those who operate above systems of justice. It could deliver needed accountability to invisibly-corrupt areas of society.

mith
@ManInTheHoody

the biggest difference between corporations and people is that america wont let corporations die

Chapter 48

Debt Jubilee

Ending The Federal Reserve Abuse of Public Power For Private Enrichment

<u>This Chapter is about:</u>   Two possible solutions to reset a 100 year old rigged game.

<u>It is important because:</u> Bad belief systems are tremendous opportunities for change...if we truly wish a better world.

Imagine if two "rights" could address Trillions of "wrongs".

What if the game of easy money for some persons, but not for others, could be reset to restore fairness in society?

The only ways out of private **debt** are to pay it, default, or have it forgiven with a **Debt Jubilee**. Wikipedia

In Jewish Mosaic Law, every seventh Sabbath year saw the wiping away of all **debts**, where creditors cancelled all the obligations of **their** fellow Israelites. Every 49th year (seven Sabbath years) was the 'Year of the **Jubilee**' when freedom from all **debt** and servitude was proclaimed throughout the land
https://www.telegraph.co.uk/finance/economics/11383374/The-biggest-debt-write-offs-in-the-history-of-the-world.html

---

Given that money creators, bankers, politicians, lawyers etc., have rigged the financial game for hundreds of years, it is probably only fair that the game be reset, to restore a level playing field.

Here is how Sweden and Norway did it in 1931:

How Swedes and Norwegians Broke the Power of the '1 Percent'

While many of us work to create a better world, it's worthwhile to consider other countries where masses of people succeeded in nonviolently bringing about a high degree of democracy and economic justice. Sweden and Norway, for example, both experienced a major power shift in the 1930s after prolonged nonviolent struggle. They "fired" the top 1 percent of people who set the direction for society and created the basis for something different.

Both countries had a history of horrendous poverty. When the 1 percent was in charge, hundreds of thousands of people emigrated to avoid starvation. Under the leadership of the working class, however, both countries built robust and successful economies that nearly eliminated poverty, expanded free university education, abolished slums, provided excellent health care available to all as a matter of right and created a system of full employment. Unlike the Norwegians, the Swedes didn't find oil, but that didn't stop them from building what the latest CIA World Factbook calls "an enviable standard of living."

Swedes and Norwegians paid a price for their standards of living through nonviolent struggle. There was a time when Scandinavian workers didn't expect that the electoral arena could deliver the change they believed in. They realized that, with the 1 percent in charge, electoral "democracy" was stacked against them, so nonviolent direct action was needed to exert the power for change.

When workers formed unions in the early 1900s, they generally turned to Marxism, organizing for revolution as well as immediate gains. They were overjoyed by the overthrow of the czar in Russia, and the Norwegian Labor Party joined the Communist International organized by Lenin. Labor didn't stay long, however. One way in which most Norwegians parted ways with Leninist strategy was on the role of violence: Norwegians wanted to win their revolution through collective nonviolent struggle, along with establishing co-ops and using the electoral arena.

In the 1920s strikes increased in intensity. The town of Hammer-
fest formed a commune in 1921, led by workers councils; the army
intervened to crush it. The workers' response verged toward a national general strike. The employers, backed by the state, beat
back that strike, but workers erupted again in the ironworkers'
strike of 1923–24.

The Norwegian 1 percent decided not to rely simply on the army;
in 1926 they formed a social movement called the Patriotic
League, recruiting mainly from the middle class. By the 1930s, the
League included as many as 100,000 people for armed protection
of strike breakers—this in a country of only 3 million!

The Labor Party, in the meantime, opened its membership to anyone, whether or not in a unionized workplace. Middle-class Marx-
ists and some reformers joined the party. Many rural farm workers
joined the Labor Party, as well as some small landholders. Labor
leadership understood that in a protracted struggle, constant out-
reach and organizing was needed to a nonviolent campaign. In
the midst of the growing polarization, Norway's workers launched
another wave of strikes and boycotts in 1928.

The Depression hit bottom in 1931. More people were jobless
there than in any other Nordic country. Unlike in the U.S., the
Norwegian union movement kept the people thrown out of work as
members, even though they couldn't pay dues. This decision paid
off in mass mobilizations. When the employers' federation locked
employees out of the factories to try to force a reduction of wages,
the workers fought back with massive demonstrations.

Many people then found that their mortgages were in jeopardy.
(Sound familiar?) The Depression continued, and farmers were
unable to keep up payment on their debts. As turbulence hit the
rural sector, crowds gathered nonviolently to prevent the eviction
of families from their farms. The Agrarian Party, which included
larger farmers and had previously been allied with the Conservative Party, began to distance itself from the 1 percent; some could
see that the ability of the few to rule the many was in doubt.

By 1935, Norway was on the brink. The Conservative-led government was losing legitimacy daily; the 1 percent became increas-

ingly desperate as militancy grew among workers and farmers. A complete overthrow might be just a couple years away, radical workers thought. However, the misery of the poor became more urgent daily, and the Labor Party felt increasing pressure from its members to alleviate their suffering, which it could do only if it took charge of the government in a compromise agreement with the other side.

This it did. In a compromise that allowed owners to retain the right to own and manage their firms, Labor in 1935 took the reins of government in coalition with the Agrarian Party. They expanded the economy and started public works projects to head toward a policy of full employment that became the keystone of Norwegian economic policy. Labor's success and the continued militancy of workers enabled steady inroads against the privileges of the 1 percent, to the point that majority ownership of all large firms was taken by the public interest. (There is an entry on this case as well at the Global Nonviolent Action Database.)

The 1 percent thereby lost its historic power to dominate the economy and society. Not until three decades later could the Conservatives return to a governing coalition, having by then accepted the new rules of the game, including a high degree of public ownership of the means of production, extremely progressive taxation, strong business regulation for the public good and the virtual abolition of poverty. When Conservatives eventually tried a fling with neoliberal policies, the economy generated a bubble and headed for disaster. (Sound familiar?)

Labor stepped in, seized the three largest banks, fired the top management, left the stockholders without a dime and refused to bail out any of the smaller banks. The well-purged Norwegian financial sector was not one of those countries that lurched into crisis in 2008; carefully regulated and much of it publicly owned, the sector was solid.

Although Norwegians may not tell you about this the first time you meet them, the fact remains that their society's high level of freedom and broadly-shared prosperity began when workers and farmers, along with middle-class allies, waged a nonviolent struggle that empowered the people to govern for the common good.

With gratitude for the excerpts gratefully used above, from films-foraction.org, please support the good works that they do on behalf of the public interest. They are trying to make the world better for all of us.

https://www.filmsforaction.org/articles/how-swedes-and-norwegians-broke-the-power-of-the-1-percent/?fbclid=IwAR395ea7m-N_T-1zLf22qGJP3XI5biNStatPX6hRGN3gUkTA6L9fNiAIzV48

Today (2020) Norway is one of the more civil countries in the world, and has a Sovereign wealth fund (belonging to citizens instead of corporations) of over one Trillion Dollars, the largest such fund in the world. In less advanced countries, billionaires absconded with money like this, rather than let it benefit society.

Is it because Norway stayed out of the European Union?

Norway–European Union relations. Norway is not a member state of the European Union (EU). ... Norway had considered joining the European Community and the European Union twice, but opted to decline following referendums in 1972 and 1994.

Wikipedia

When I compare it (Norway's fund) to a similar sovereign resource fund that was bigger, and begun prior to Norway's fund, in Alberta, Canada, the comparison stings. Alberta's oil wealth fund has shown zero growth in the last few decades. It remains in the same range of between ten to twenty Billion that it was in the 1970's, while Norway's fund has gone from Zero dollars to over One Trillion dollars during that same time. We Canadians, politicians and cronies blew it for our own selfish ends, while Norway took the high road.

I don't have anything against Billionaires, so long as they made billions by honest work and contribution to the economy. That is what Adam Smith meant by the "invisible hand" that guides men to do what is best for other men…and be rewarded for doing so.

But when billions are made by unfairness, cheating and by taking advantage of a rigged game, that is a different story. That is "Rentier Games". Then we are talking about billions made not by helping others, but by commodifying them and extracting their wealth.

The above-human powers granted to Corporations has given a small number of men the power to get away with unfairness and do harm to other humans. They have the "I did not do it, my invisible friend (the corporation) did", excuse.

Perhaps it is time for a game reset. Perhaps we need to revisit the unfairness of the lawyer created belief system that we call the Corporation, and what it has done to society. If certain people have benefitted from an unfair belief system, perhaps we should reset that particular belief system and restore fairness to society.

Corporations have received debt forgiveness (bailouts) over and over again, so they are not new. Perhaps it is time to drop that "helicopter money" upon ordinary humans…to be fair. Corporations have also benefitted from over a Century of limited liability, and limited ability to prosecute or hold them accountable, whereas ordinary men (those who do not own or control a corporation) have not had such advantages. This has allowed corporate owners to gain tremendous wealth and power over ordinary members of the public. This "more equal" status of the corporation should not persist in an "all men are created equal" world.

One possibility to level the playing field is:

(Helicopter Money)
Helicopter drop is an expansionary fiscal policy that is financed by an increase in a economy's money supply. It could be an increase in spending or a tax cut, but it involves printing large sums of money and distributing it to the public in order to stimulate the economy. Mostly, the term 'helicopter drop' is largely a metaphor for unconventional measures to jump start the economy during deflationary periods.

While 'helicopter drop' was first mentioned by noted economist Milton Friedman, it gained popularity after Ben Bernanke made a passing reference to it in a November 2002 speech, when he was a new Federal Reserve governor. That single reference earned

Bernanke the sobriquet of 'Helicopter Ben', a nickname that stayed with him during much of his tenure as a Fed member and Fed chairman.

Investopedia

If something is odious, it's hateful. If you become a historian of slavery, you'll learn all the details of that odious trade. Odious is from the Latin noun odium, which means hatred. It is a strong word, so don't call someone odious unless you want to accuse someone of being loathsome or vile. Odious debts are those incurred upon a people, country or society by despots or dictators.

In international law, odious debt, also known as illegitimate debt, is a legal theory that says that the national debt incurred by a despotic regime shall not be enforceable. I suggest that the trillions of debt placed upon the backs of American taxpayers, to funnel cash to just a few hands, should be an unenforceable debt, or at very least those billionaire recipients should be pursued with RICO and proceeds of crime confiscation.

If banks and giant corporations are not subject to the laws of ordinary people, then the question could be asked if ordinary people should be subject to laws at all. Are laws even legitimate if they are not applied fairly? Are public systems which are unfair or corrupt by definition, deserving of public respect? Asking for a friend. Americans sure felt this way when it was Britain that was farming them 240 years ago.

What if a Debt Jubilee for non-corporate persons and non-corporate debt were a way to deal with entities that:

a) hold themselves above the law, or have risen to a rigged "above-law" status,
b) are too big to jail,
c) are self policing,
d) appear to own or control the government for the benefit of a few rather than of the public
e) are further protected by corporate limited liability
f) are unaccountable to the public

g)   are less than 100% transparent to society

I may be dreaming, but there are signs today that printing trillions of dollars and "gifting" much of it to banks, while burdening Americans with the debt, might justify a debt jubilee for non-corporate entities (humans persons only) to restore fairness. Average Americans should not have to shoulder the debt, and pay the tax to fund the debt, just so that nearly free money can be given away to billionaires and banks can collect more interest. North Americans (and others) are being looted to a point which is literally killing it's economic heartbeat. Humans, not artificial persons, are the economic heartbeat.

==========

60% of Germany's debt was "forgiven" in The London Agreement of 1953. What a kind gesture when the debt of a nation becomes odious and/or dangerous to society. Sadly Germany would not return the same kindness to Greece, during the Greek crisis in more recent years. (2009)

During 1932-39, average debt relief amounted to 19% of national output in advanced economies, according to economists Carmen Reinhart and Christoph Tresbech.

For the likes of France and Greece, the Jubilees were closer to 50% and 40% of GDP respectively.

Full repayment was so rare, that Finland was the sole European sovereign who managed to honor all its post-war obligations.

Germany's post-war economic miracle
Only 16% of polled Germans currently think Greece should be the recipient of some form of debt cancellation from the eurozone. The irony of Berlin's obstinance on debt relief may well be lost on some.
Following the end of WWII, the London Debt Agreement of 1953 saw the abolition of all of Germany's external debt. The total for-

giveness amounted to around 280% of GDP from 1947-53, according to historian Albrecht Ritschl.

https://www.telegraph.co.uk/finance/economics/11383374/The-biggest-debt-write-offs-in-the-history-of-the-world.html

The image below portrays the share of economic lifeblood that drains away to a criminal class of Rentiers who have rigged our systems from above, verses the share of public resources that go to benefit society.

This is what 21st Century slavery looks like. Give the right to create money out of thin air to a small group, and in 100 years they will own everything...and everyone.

Outstanding Student Loan Debt Approaches $1.5
https://www.bloomberg.com/news/articles/2018-11-
16/student-debt-onus-approaching-1-5-trillion-
demographic-trends?cmpid=socialflow-twitter-
business&utm_source=twitter&utm_content=business&utm
_medium=social&utm_campaign=socialflow-organic

BLOOMBERG.COM
Outstanding Student Loan Debt Approaches $1.5 Trillion
Outstanding student loan debt increased by $37 billion in the third...

Chapter 49

The Accountability Movement
A new Industry of Accountability

<u>This Chapter is about:</u>   Dreams of a new industry of accountability, intended to rebuild fairness, justice and rule of law where those principles have been eroded.

<u>It is important because:</u>   I believe accountability is one of the key ingredients in a free and safe society and I believe it was destroyed through some of the dirty tricks described in this book.

I don't dream about saving the environment.

I dream about several environments.
Those I dream about are:

1.   The *natural environment* we live in:

2. The *social environment* we share, which includes levels of world co-operation, peace in the world, and peace in your neighborhood.

3. The *economic environment* that is shared by every living thing on the planet. The share of economic resources, like finance, food, safety and and shelter is a huge factor in how we live together socially and in peace.

4. The *"professional and public servant"* environment.

I dream of these environments, since each is connected to the health of humanity, of society and of the planet.

Part of the solution is:
1. Something that I call the "Accountability Movement" or the "New Industry of Accountability". A fair question next might be to ask, "What is the Accountability Movement?"

Whistleblowers risk everything to warn the public of disaster, while public servants and people in power place entire society's at risk to gain personal benefits for themselves. This is a classic breach of their duties and a criminal breach of the public trust.

Roger Mark Boisjoly was an American mechanical engineer, fluid dynamicist, and an aerodynamicist. He is best known for having raised strenuous objections to the launch of the Space Shuttle Challenger months before the loss of the spacecraft and its crew in January 1986. He died as a broken man due to the retaliation against him for having dared to save peoples lives…by questioning those above him in positions of power. (Remember that the unwritten principles or rules of gravity, prevent application of power *upwards*)

Billions of eyeballs could be acting as public watchdogs upon power, in a fair, safe, honest society. $100 Million dollars in reward incentives for society watchdogs would be "thousands of a penny", when divided among the Trillions being looted from society by those above.

Today we live in a world where most so-called "watchdogs" are government or private corporate powers, Many of these powers pretend to be public servants while they monitor and spy on public citizens. Trillions of dollars are lost to society with the help of these wolves dressed as watchdogs. I hope readers will not take my word for any of this, but will do their own research. The kind of life your children will be allowed to live depends on what you do today to prepare it for them.

"What sets whistleblowers apart is they're able to continue to walk forward knowing that everyone's turning against them," he (Zeno Franco) told CBC Go Public's Erica Johnson.
"Stubborn-ness in that situation is actually a strength. It's in their DNA in that sense. They can't help but call us back to account."
"Whistleblowers ... [are] almost more heroic than somebody that's running into a burning building. The process unfolds over time and the whistleblower has multiple opportunities to withdraw. "

The World Justice Project's definition of the rule of law is comprised of the following four universal principles:
1. Accountability
The government as well as private actors are accountable under the law.

2. Just Laws
The laws are clear, publicized, and stable; are applied evenly; and protect fundamental rights, including the security of persons and contract, property, and human rights.

3. Open Government
The processes by which the laws are enacted, administered, and enforced are accessible, fair, and efficient. Citizen Assembly's.

4. Accessible & Impartial Dispute Resolution
Justice is delivered timely by competent, ethical, and independent representatives and neutrals who are accessible, have adequate resources, and reflect the makeup of the communities they serve.

https://worldjusticeproject.org/about-us/overview/what-rule-law

The Accountability Movement dreams of financial rewards for whistleblowers and Truth tellers. Those are individuals who protect the public interest by reporting public interest wrongdoings by any entity that is responsible to protect and/or serve the public. That sounds like a police role, but it is truly the promised role of every public servant. I would like to make it an opportunity for every member of the public. No more "trust me" games where we assume that public servants will serve the public. We can do this better ourselves and create a robust prosperity at the same time. That is my hope.

It could operate like the privately funded Nobel Peace Prize, with a pool of capital acquired through donation, held by a responsible institution, (not by me although I would very much like to be involved in non-financial ways). For as little as $100 Million dollars I believe such a project could be run with the potential to change the world.

Accountability is #1 my list of things that I believe have been lost, reversed, or turned upside down by those power.

============

I believe than an "Accountability Movement" is as vital to the social fabric of our world as an Environmental Protection movement has become to our Planet. It is a priority item on my wish list of most important systemic changes needed in our world today.

Instead of crashing society, I hope we can consider new systems of accountability. A new economic-booster based upon all citizens being incentivized or rewarded to become everyday heroes?

The environmental protection industry has sprung from nothing in my lifetime, and its benefits spring from "doing well by doing good". This is a model that works. Doing well by doing good… contains little or no downside to society.

The Accountability Movement could, in my estimation, reward, encourage, and eventually employ people who could be doing good things for society. It is as essential to our social environment as clean air and water is to our physical environment.

Imagine a world where your next role could be to work as a person who helps rebuild accountability in our society. If Rosa Parks, a part time department store seamstress, could change the world in 1955, without using an iPhone, then no one among us has any excuse today.

From the FaceBook group titled "Industry of Accountability": Please Join this Accountability Movement

We seek to connect with those who believe that the greatest act we can do for each other is to demonstrate kindness, rather than selfishness or cruelty.

Knowing that the kindest act we can demonstrate at times is to stand up for the truth, no matter who tells it, or who may be opposed to it.

Realizing that to tell the truth in a world filled with lies, sometimes requires the greatest level of courage.

Those who can find this level of courage, are those whose voices are free, and un-owned by another.

Will you join us in a search for the freedom, and the courage, to tell the truth. To bring increased kindness and prosperity to all, rather than just ourselves?

https://www.facebook.com/groups/IndustryofAccountability/

The Accountability Movement could act as a billion eyes upon governments, corporations and those in power or public service.

Abuse such as employment abuse, financial abuse, corporate abuse, legal abuse, government abuse, environmental abuse. Any area where powerful people, systems or institutions do harm is of interest to the Accountability Movement.

The Accountability Movement is not intended as a replacement for the Justice system, but rather a public protective movement that systems of government cannot provide. Or as my friend Joe often says, modern day systems of power have been hijacked, often by the very people running the systems, who have learned how to gain personal advantage from those systems. Systems always seem to feed the system before public interest considerations.

Whistleblowers, truth tellers, financial protection, justice, environmental protection, etc., all and more, will be welcome areas where unchecked power and accountability might benefit from having eyes of public oversight looking into them.

What potential could exist if we could annually award between ten and twenty financial prizes, "Accountability Awards" of $100,000 each, to ten or twenty of society's everyday-heroes? How about billions of dollars in cost savings, crime savings, corruption reduction and rewards for society-benefitting work? That is a potential, hundred-fold return to society. Imagine potentially turning things around for pennies on the dollar? Take the televised ratings extravaganza that surrounded shows like "American Idol", and make a similar hit ratings program based on Everyday Hero's. *Again, doing well by doing good.*

=========

The Accountability Movement (Industry of Accountability) hopes to become a beacon of hope to millions who otherwise suffer in silence.

EVERYDAY HERO AWARDS

Got a secret about corrupt government or corporate bad behavior? Is it big enough to tell the world about it? Does it involve systemic harm to millions, or private illegal gain in the billions? Why not consider documenting it (if you are in that position) and submitting it to an awards committee for recognition and reward? Systemic issues that affect all of society will be of interest to the industry of accountability, or the accountability movement.

We will keep it confidential unless it is an award winning submission, and then, only with your express permission. Perhaps this will allow you to follow your own conscience, help humanity in your own way, and capture one of the coolest global prizes on the planet, The Accountability Movement <u>EVERYDAY HERO AWARD!!</u>

============

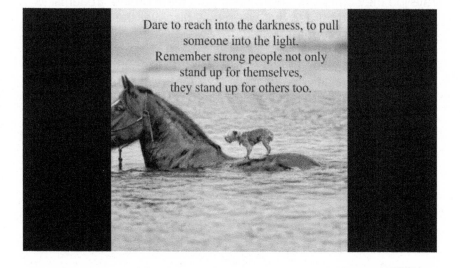

Dare to reach into the darkness, to pull someone into the light.
Remember strong people not only stand up for themselves, they stand up for others too.

CHAPTER 50

Crimes Against Humanity
Hidden Quid Pro Quo's

This Chapter is about: Lets teach the world about systemic literacy.

It is important because: Children are growing up never being given the tools to protect themselves and their society from the secret games that play out beneath the game.

I believe that a new subject area of financial and political literacy is needed. One where young minds are schooled in areas which organized professionals and public servants do not want the public to know. Many fields, social sciences, finance, psychology, politics and economics come into play in this area and I think it would be a fascinating new field to understand better.

The universities of today have business schools which seem to churn out minds with little opportunity but to take the first corporate job they can land. This merely puts them on the treadmill to be used up and burned out, when they discover the soul extraction side of the corporate world.

Little chance is given to find jobs which add to GDP or to human happiness. Business grads must fight for the scraps of employment, which include working for a corporation which does little but harvest the GDP of a country. Finance, and the million handmaids to finance, have assumed this extraction role in society.

=======

The easiest thing to do is to reward a human's self-instincts for self-preservation. Human instincts will grasp that "self" interested reward, even if it hurts millions of people.

A sad discovery yes. Am I immune from those instincts of self preservation? No. I have each human trait and every instinctual human failing. But I am working on them.

I am perhaps the luckiest man in the world, in that I was allowed to see the inner criminal workings of my industry at a time in my life when I still had my childish beliefs in principles and professionalism.

I am also lucky because I got the ability to choose my own struggle. I got to choose the hill I was willing to die on, (so to speak:). Many do not get that luxury, Many others are caught in traps in which they had no part in choosing.

Look today at how many millions of people are caught in a trap of poverty, fear and desperation, while some members of society float-freely above the laws of gravity. (or above the laws) They can get away with almost anything, while the police chase the "little people", who must work, fight or steal to survive in a rigged world. I think it may be the hidden design, behind our society. I don't know for sure, but I am trying to understand.

The following image and quote from Tara Brach speaks to me of the pain and suffering that I see among the public in many developed countries today. I sympathize and am trying to do what I can to understand the systemic causes. Too many people are caught in a place of vulnerability and pain, due to no fault of their own, when corporations and billionaires have invisible and unfair advantages. Not enough people are talking about the unfairness. I hope to have an effect on that.

"Imagine you are walking in the woods and you see a small dog sitting by a tree. As you approach it, it suddenly lunges at you, teeth bared. You are frightened and angry. But then you notice that one of its legs is caught in a trap. Immediately your mood shifts from anger to concern: You see that the dog's aggression is coming from a place of vulnerability and pain. This applies to all of us. When we behave in hurtful ways, it is because we are caught in some kind of trap. The more we look through the eyes of wisdom at ourselves and one another, the more we cultivate a compassionate heart."

~TARA BRACH

Chapter 51

500BC
First Democracy and Citizen Assembly

This Chapter is about: Imagine if there were no "professional" politicians to corrupt?

It is important because: It is too simple not to consider.

From the book, "First Democracy", comes the story of how the Greeks learned to take the virus of corruption, politics and influence- peddling out of their systems of governance. They learned this the hard way, by trial and error over many years. Sadly we have forgotten, or certain elite classes have intentionally fooled us...so they could farm us.

The Greeks had a process where government decisions were made by ordinary citizens, who were temporarily selected to serve as public officials for a day. No professional politicians were needed and this was learned after much trial and error by the Greeks.

Their citizen governance model was like a jury-selection process where members of the public serve as jurors to hear a legal case and help the courts arrive at unbiased decisions for the community. The use of volunteer citizens, or citizens paid to serve in temporary positions eliminated the effects of cronyism and conflicts of interest that arise when public servants become too comfortable with their positions of power and influence.

They eliminated the opportunity for thousands of corruption-causing virus's to infect their systems of governance, by eliminating the carrier that is "professional politicians".
What a brilliant solution that is worth discovery.

Americans have an unwavering faith in democracy and are ever eager to import it to nations around the world. But how democratic is our own "democracy"? If you can vote, if the majority rules, if you have elected representatives--does this automatically mean that you have a democracy? In this eye-opening look at an ideal that we all take for granted, classical scholar Paul Woodruff offers some surprising answers to these questions.

Drawing on classical literature, philosophy, and history--with many intriguing passages from Sophocles, Aesop, and Plato, among others--Woodruff immerses us in the world of ancient Athens to uncover how the democratic impulse first came to life.

The heart of the book isolates seven conditions that are the sine qua non of democracy: freedom from tyranny , harmony, the rule of law, natural equality, citizen wisdom, reasoning without knowledge, and general education. He concludes that a true democracy must be willing to invite everyone to join in government.

It must respect the rule of law so strongly that even the government is not above the law. True democracy must be mature enough to accept changes that come from the people. And it must be willing to pay the price of education for thoughtful citizenship. If we learn anything from the story of Athens, Woodruff concludes, it should be this--never lose sight of the ideals of democracy. This compact, eloquent book illuminates these ideals and lights the way as we struggle to keep democracy alive at home and around the world.

https://www.amazon.ca/First-Democracy-Challenge-Ancient-Idea/dp/0195304543

Chapter 52

Life On The Edge

The Information Fringes

This Chapter is about: Getting your news, like your fresh vegetables, on the outer edges and not in the middle aisle.

It is important because: The middle and the mainstream contains the junk that is bad for you.

When a visually impaired person uses a white cane while walking, they often tap the cane from side to side, on the edges of the pathway. They do this not to test where to step, but to constantly monitor and discover where it _may not be safe_ to step. Only by discovering the fringes of safety, can they envision where the path is.

There is a similar analogy with regard to finding the truth, the safe path of knowing what is going on in society, and to keep yourself from falling for the many traps that are laid out to trip people along the way.

The analogy is that there appears to be a "mainstream" of news and information which has become fixated on one priority, and sadly the priority is no longer news. It is stimulation, distraction and political or corporate promotion. It is now more greed driven to farm its audience for profit, than to inform them.

With that in mind, humans can be said to be visually impaired, or see things distorted, redacted or even upside down. Farming humans is dependent upon fooling humans. "Pulling the wool over their eyes", is a term used to illustrate how easy it is to fool people by blinding them to truth.

The mainstream of news and information has thus become the less-safe path today in many cases. It has become a commercially captured stream. In some countries there are public broadcasting entities, which are doing their best to resist the pull of money and power. Sadly these entities, the only ones able to tell of some truths, are on the extinction-list of those addicted to money and power.

The public is thus forced further onto the "fringes", in order to seek out information which is not captured and corrupted by politics, advertising, or corporate money. The truth is still out there, but the searcher for truth must walk closer and closer to the edges, in order to find a safe path or a path of truth. Mainstream media today is no longer about informing humans, but about harvesting humans.

Personal discoveries I can warn others of:

If you are seeing anything advertised on TV claiming to be a health, financial or other benefit to the listener, it is almost 100% safe to assume the opposite is true. In other words, it's need to be advertised on that particular medium (TV) is an indicator that it is of *little real value*. *You are not the user of TV. TV is the user of you*. Systemic literacy requires you to constantly know the difference between when you are using a tool, and when you are in fact the tool that is being used...it is not always obvious.

An Agnotologist observation is that the less advertisements found in your source of information, the greater the potential for truth, or for objectivity. The reason for this is that TV programming is not here to benefit you, you are there for TV advertisers benefit. This is why you will see literally dozens of commercials about safe retirement or investing on popular programs. Financial firms pay a lot of money to get their "sales" message in front of your eyes. (remember that "sales" is not involved in "best" advice and "best" advice does not involve sales in its delivery)

If any media were to tell the whole truth, or try to warn you about bad products, it would receive far less or even zero advertising dollars.

Obtaining some of your information from outer fringes, is a good thing. I always know I have "arrived" at a fringe source of information when there are less advertisers for the media. Especially if there are less giant corporate advertisers appearing with the media. That is a clue that you have found something truly independent...(or just bad programming, you decide:).

Please note, that the absence of advertisers does not guarantee that the information presented is sound...or even sane. There are some interesting nut-jobs on the fringes. It does, however indicate a less commercially-biased message or point of view.

The above is similar to common advice about investing and shopping advice for food nutrition. Both tasks, if done well, will have you choosing food, investments, and some of your information sources from the fringes. Fringes being:

— outside center supermarket aisles for food,

—outside mega banks and life insurance companies for investments, and

—outside mainstream media, for less conflicted news or information.

If you want real, safe, true, or nutritious, you sometimes find it closer to the fringes.

Chapter 53

Anarchy, Or A New Beginning?

<u>This Chapter is about:</u> If a time comes when there are only crimi-
nals in power, will there be anything to do but to disobey?

<u>It is important because:</u> Will that be anarchy, or a new beginning?

Anarchy is the state of a society being freely constituted without
authorities or a governing body. It may also refer to a society or
group of people that totally rejects a set hierarchy. The word anarchy was first used in 1539, meaning "an absence of government". Wikipedia

---

Anarchy seems to be the no-rules-apply, operating system of
wealthiest class of power and money players. One solution to level the playing field might be for the rest to simply ignore lawless
capitalism where it is found.

What about asking the very simple question: "If this _____
(rule, law, tax, obligation or confiscation) does not apply fairly
upon everyone, then why does it apply to me, and is it even legitimate?"

By "legitimate", I do not mean, does the "power" or authority who
is imposing the rule, law, tax, obligation or confiscation, have
some legalized paper-given right to do so? Of course they do. But
is it right?

Is it legitimate when the legalized, politically driven or corporate
sponsored "power" sells or gives away the fair treatment of the
public, in order to create advantages to themselves, or to private
or corporate interests? This is generally thought of as Breach of
the Public Trust, or Racketeering under RICO statutes.

If the answer to the question, "is it even legitimate" is no, and if the issue is something of importance to all people (systemic), then it is fair to ask if it must be followed by those in a free society?

If any "system" that we allow in our society is:

1. Unfair
2. Unaccountable to the public
3. Not 100% transparent to the public, or
4. Not responsible for improving the public good
5. Contains special treatment, secrecy, confidentiality

Is it even legitimate, or should it be questioned, tested and challenged continually? Should it exist if it cannot meet the test of full open public accountability?

I make no recommendations in this book how people should behave, but I do observe that many times in history, people who have suffered long enough under rigged and predatory systems of oppression, have simply stood up, and said no. What if people simply behave as if there is no leader...when there is no proven legitimate leadership?

Passed in 1970, the Racketeer Influenced and Corrupt Organizations Act (RICO) is a federal law designed to combat organized crime in the United States. It allows prosecution and civil penalties for racketeering activity performed as part of an ongoing criminal enterprise.

To convict a defendant under RICO, the government must prove that the defendant engaged in two or more instances of racketeering activity and that the defendant directly invested in, maintained an interest in, or participated in a criminal enterprise affecting interstate or foreign commerce.

The good news is that this act may apply to enough political actors that by its enforcement the country could be cleansed of corruption. The bad news is that government prosecutors do not typically prosecute governments...or the powerful. All the more reason for some publicly driven Accountability Movements.

Private prosecution
From Wikipedia, the free encyclopedia

A private prosecution is a criminal proceeding initiated by an individual or private organization (such as a prosecution association) instead of by a public prosecutor who represents the state. Private prosecutions are allowed in many jurisdictions under common law, but have become less frequent in modern times as most prosecutions are now handled by professional public prosecutors instead of private individuals who retain (or are themselves) barristers.

Canada and the U.S. allow private citizens to file criminal charges without the need for a lawyer, policeman or prosecutor. Check it out as one of the possible avenues of public recourse when authorities cannot prosecute anything more powerful than themselves.

I WISH...

How do we get beyond a "Me, Me, Me", society, professionally rigged to the point of lawlessness, into a "we" society? Or even just a fair society, instead of a rigged game.

How do we restore some degree of law and order?

Some things I wish for in no particular order:

I wish we would consider jail for professional accountants who specialize in tax-eliminating accounting tricks. I recall decades ago learning that the amount of man hours of labour spent (wasted?) doing income tax preparation was greater than the man hours of productive labour spent manufacturing every car built in America. I do not know how it compares today, but there are less cars manufactured in America these days, and more accounting tricks.

I wish there was a simple 30% flat tax on any income over 30K.

No exceptions, no shelters for corporations, No exemptions, No accounting tricks. Simply put every income on the same standard. The savings in costing inefficiency to any country would be hundreds of billions, and the smartest accountants and lawyers could go forth and engage in work of a productive nature, rather than detracting from the economy.

I wish there were Whistleblower rewards, for revealing hidden or offshore assets, to encourage whistleblowing and discourage hiding money from your country. To hide money from the country that gave a person or corporation its prosperity, is a criminal act which attempts to benefit from the country while not contributing or paying into it. Right now this kind of criminal act is a professional sport, aided by bankers, lawyers and accountants. I would like to see everyday citizens, even ethical professionals rewarded with 10% of any money they help recover by going public. That would be a win for the public, and a win for the whistleblower.

Today we have networks of organized financial professionals who are paid billions to help hide and launder Trillions. We are literally building entire industries of "professionals" who personally gain by doing harm to society. Again RICO comes to mind.

I wish I could teach financial literacy in school, as well as University courses in Agnotology and Systemic Financial and Political Literacy. North Americans are being permanently scammed by experts in scamming the public. I think this could be one of the new ways to create a safer society.

As part of teaching our children about systemic financial and political literacy, lets teach them what a Rentier economy looks like, and help them learn what the term "rent seeking" truly means.

I wish there were a basic "guaranteed minimum income" to support the most vulnerable members of a society. If we were to add up the bailouts to banks, subsidies to other corporations ,and the money printing franchise gifted to the privately owned Federal Reserve, it becomes clear that corporations have had a "guaranteed maximum income" for over 100 years now. It has benefitted them by Trillions of dollars and every penny comes at the expense of society.

(it bears repeating that every dollar the Fed ever created was backed by U.S. debt piled upon the backs of U.S. taxpayers. The Fed owners get trillions in private benefit and U.S. citizens pay for it…please correct me if I am mistaken in my understanding)

A basic income guarantee would provide each citizen with a sum of money. Except for citizenship, a basic income is entirely uncon-ditional.
A basic income guarantee would simplify or end the welfare state, might balance out the "maximum guaranteed income" that corpo-rations and Fed Bankers have received for 100 years, and truly ensure that no one has to live in poverty. Its necessity may be-come increasingly obvious as more human labor is replaced by machines. Imagine it like putting "water-wings" upon children be-fore letting them into the swimming pool. Some members of soci-ety are too vulnerable to be left unprotected in an unsafe environ-ment.

Today we have corporate and political collaboration which cheats the public out of the benefits of fair and honest capitalism, while providing a rigged, unlimited and unfair income to those who least need it, those with the most money, legal advantages and power.

==========

"What compels your compassion?

What is important enough to you that you would give up nearly everything, to try and make it happen? For me it is the wish for my children to live in a free world. The valuable part of this wish is the realization that for them to live in a free world, it means that I must also wish for your children to live in a free world. You and everyone else.

This person on the next page is not suffering from laziness. This person is suffering from unfairness. I know many people like this and it is not fair to automatically apply a "lazy" label upon those less fortunate. Your children or grandchildren might get the opportunity to experience this for themselves, unless we stand up against unfair acts.

Remember, what the older folks told you: "what goes around, comes around."

Is this person suffering from weakness…or unfairness?

In summary, this book has hope for the following.

Hoped-for belief system changes to stop Farming Humans:

1. Investigate and address the "lawless" aspect of what is now "lawless capitalism" at the top. Recovery of proceeds of financial crime should be a priority, and an entirely new industry.

2. An "Accountability Movement" could be as important to the future of society as environmental protection has become to our planet, and could be what is needed for #2 above.

3. Debt Jubilee for non-corporate debt (personally held debt), to address the unfairness under which Corporations and banks have been enriched for 100 years at the expense of the public. (see #1)

4. Correction of artificial social constructs, and belief systems which makes corporations and persons who own corporations above the reach of our systems of justice?

5. Citizens Assembly's like Greece 2000 years ago, or advanced societies such as New Zealand today. Professional politicians are a liability and a contradiction to what public service truly means. They are a breeding ground for pandemics of self-dealing, rot and corruption.

6. Oh,…and I almost forgot, we may need "systemic crimes trials" for systemic financial and political crimes that are committed upon the public, just like the "War Crimes" trials of old. Those persons who cheat humanity due to their own depravity must be brought to justice, otherwise we are just letting them profit.

Poverty is not an accident. Like slavery and apartheid, it is man-made and can be removed by the actions of human beings.

- Nelson Mandela

For 20 years I was a child,
For 20 more I was a slave,
For 20 years I tried to grow up,
For 20 years I now repay.
-- Larry Elford

End of Book
Beginning of The Journey

Some Possible Action Steps For Readers To Consider

1. Pass this book along to someone, to help them become financially aware and systemically street smart.

2. Better yet, buy three books and make sure your three closest friends get a copy… (self-interested sales pitch:)

3. Send a copy to a charitable foundation or philanthropist who is engaged in improving the world, and let's make the Accountability Movement a real thing. Is there a modern-day Alfred Nobel out there who wishes to give the world a better chance? I don't care to handle or touch the money, but I can picture helping the vision happen with the right people.

4. Begin teaching financial literacy in schools, and more important, <u>systemic</u> corruption and financial and political literacy.

5. Learn and teach the concepts of Agnotology. It is a required skill in a world of misinformation.

6. Join the Facebook Group titled "Investment System Fraud" and help make the world a financially safer place.

7. Follow @RecoveredBroker on Twitter

8. Join the "Industry of Accountability" group on Facebook, and lets change the world, by using social media for social good.

9. Join a Facebook group called Debt Jubilee (forgiveness, reset,...or collapse) to find out more about giving the financial game a "fairness reset".

10. Visit investoradvocates.ca and learn how to get your money back from falsely-represented financial advisors.

11. Several statutes, mostly codified in Title 18 of the United States Code, provide for federal prosecution of public corruption in the United States. Sec 122 Breach of Trust in Canada is the criminal offense for much of the corruption found in this book, and in society.

12. Privately filed criminal charges are allowed by any citizen, against public servants and officials who sell out the public interest. (see "Civil or Criminal Actions against companies or regulators" at www.investoradvocates.ca)

13. Citizen Public Inquiries should be encouraged and welcomed, to ensure that the public never places 100% trust and reliance upon power structures alone. Relying on power to be it's own police over power, is naive and dangerous to society.

14. Consider actions against power and authority who abuse power and authority for self-enrichment. Refuse to obey (#OptOut) of any unfair, unjust, rigged or corrupt government authority, policy etc. Act as if it #AintThere if it #AintFair. This might be your only true choice remaining.

15. Visit the Facebook group, Canadian Justice Review Board, and help those who are hoping to make the system better.

16. Someone please build a "Facebook-like" social media platform with public service as its underlying theme, and without the corporate ownership, profit seeking, human farming backing and underwriting.

17. Start your own "Citizens Assembly" wherever you are. Allow it to play, "Let's pretend we want the very best for our friends, family and society" and "Let's pretend we are objective, un-conflicted bystanders". https://thespinoff.co.nz/atea/23-11-2019/who-gets-to-be-an-ordinary-new-zealander-on-citizens-assemblies-climate-change-and-tangata-whenua/

18. Let's pretend that citizens are the masters of a free country, and the public servants are,…wait for it….the servants. Lets hold them accountable to serve, and not to rule.

19. Let's discuss like philosophers, in order to find underlying principles, and let's focus less on personalities, labels and name calling.

20. Consider that the Thirty Dirty Tricks in this book to Farm Humans are forms of violence upon you and yours, and let's see what we can do to stop violent people or practices from running or ruining society.

21. Spot the psychopaths, the sycophants and the sickness they cause in our world.

22. Society is not falling apart because we cannot arrest all the addicts and street criminals. Society falls apart because we arrest virtually zero of the truly serious criminals in our society. https://www.youtube.com/watch?v=H7loq7LcHLM

We need to stop just pulling people out of the river.

We need to go upstream and *find out why they're falling in.*

-Desmond Tutu

What does it mean if something is a derivative?

1. As a noun, a derivative is a kind of financial agreement or contract.

2. As an adjective, a derivative describes something that borrows heavily from something else that came before it.

3. Derivatives are a fundamental tool of calculus. (Wikipedia)

======

1. Used as a noun: A derivative is a contract between two or more parties whose value is based on an agreed-upon underlying financial asset (like a security) or set of assets (like an index). Common underlying instruments include stocks, bonds, commodities, currencies, interest rates and market indexes. www.investopedia.com

2. Used as an adjective: The kind of democracy we have today is one step removed from true democracy, this it is a derivative of democracy, and the portion that is removed is in the fair and equal standing of all people before government and the law.

========

In this book, I am using "derivative" as a metaphor or "thought experiment" to describe several things including:

Derivative News (fake news, or deliberately slanted news)
Derivative Politics (persons who pretend to be public servants)
Derivative Money (paper wealth used to represent true wealth)
Derivative Professional advice (ie, having an "advisor" instead of a licensed fiduciary "adviser" is to have a "derivative adviser")
Derivative Democracy government with removal of principles of
           a) all citizens being equal before the law
              b) political freedom and
              c) rule of law

"What you do in your lifetime, informs the generations that come after you…"
Chris Hedges

The secret of happiness is freedom and the secret of freedom is courage.
History of the Peloponnesian War, Book II, by Thucydides (ca. 410 BC)

"Try to do what is right."
"If you are not sure what is right, then try to do what is kind."
Larry Elford

Index of Farming Human Tricks in this book.

Trick #1 for Farming Humans is the ability to invisibly commit crime. Chapter 1, Page 9, Ring of Gyges

Trick #2 for Farming Humans is to allow professionals to create rigged systems or self serving social constructs. Chapter 4, page 28 (Lawyers who serve corporate interests are often incentivized to assist in harming the society to increase their own security. SEC, Bernie Madoff, Corporations as invisible friends, Money laundering assistance)

Trick #3 in Farming Humans is making it legal for insider manipulation of public markets for private gain. (Boeing CEO) page 32

Trick #4 for Farming Humans is Justice prefers to look only down…rarely up towards power. Chapter 5, page 33.

Trick #5 for Farming Humans is "let us create the nation's money". What could go wrong? Found in Chapter 7 on page 38.

Trick # 6 in the game of Farming Humans, to create something which gives a few men an elevated status above the rest. Southern Pacific Railroad taxes, to Pacific Gas and Electric deadly California fires, to Boeing aircraft casualties. Paper "persons" cannot be arrested or jailed.

Trick #7 for Farming Humans is a private game of money creation which secretly "borrowed" on the credit backing of the public. Chapter 9, page 51. Federal Reserve.

Trick #8 for Farming Humans is seen in the removal of the gold backing of US dollars for global trading partners, a second default of the promises behind the dollar. (1971) Chapter 15, page 81

Trick #9 for Farming Humans is being able to sell out the public trust, over and over again. Supreme Court rules that money equals speech. Chapter 16, page 91.

Trick #10 for Farming Humans is Clinton repeals Glass Steagall, letting banks gamble America into yet another financial collapse. Chapter 17, page 93.

Trick #11 for Farming Humans is when money is allowed to buy politics. Citizens United, super PAC's can spend unlimited money during campaigns. Chapter 18, page 97.

Trick #12 for Farming Humans is the Derivative Revolution. Making it up with lawyers and papers in a continual game of "lets pretend". Chapter 19, page 105.

Trick #13 for Farming Humans is allowing dis-information to infect society. Chapter 20, page 109.

Trick #14 for Farming Humans is substitution of an "advisor", for what investors think is an "adviser". Confused yet? The clever "vowel movement" adds billions in profits, while farming investors.

Trick #15 for Farming Humans is when privately-hired rental-cops are allowed to lawfully regulate an industry, the public gets abused. Investments, SEC, FDA, FAA etc. Chapter 15, page 122

Trick #16 for Farming Humans is the layer of industry "self regulators", your second army of people paid to "gaslight" the public into thinking they are protected. Chapter 23, page 132.

Trick #17 for Farming Humans is using stock markets to launder taxpayer backed, Fed created money to those who control the Fed. Chapter 25, page 136.

Trick #18 for Farming Humans is the use of fake information to ensure that society never knows what is true and what is false. Elections, wars, headlines etc. Chapter 26, page 141.

Trick #19 for Farming Humans is stimulation and distraction. This emotional hacking of humans is Trick #19 for Farming Humans. See Social Engineering: The Art of Human Hacking Book by Christopher J. Hadnagy

Trick #20 for Farming Humans is the elimination of the Fairness Doctrine and 83 media regulations, including requirement for "honest, equitable and balanced". Chapter 28, page 153.

Trick #21 for Farming Humans is governments as handmaidens to corporations, not people. Chapter 29, page 157.

Trick #22 for Farming Humans is in the invisible connections between government, professionals and corporations. Chapter 31, page 162. Laws, lobby groups, lawyers.

Trick #23 for Farming Humans is a militarized police used to serve and protect power instead of people. Chapter 32, page 170. World Trade Organization, Occupy Wall Street, Black Lives Matter, etc.

Trick #24 for Farming Humans is virtually zero enforcement of crime above a certain level of money or power. Invisible friends and powerful people cannot be prosecuted. Chapter 33, page 175.

Trick #25 for Farming Humans is cooking the financial books. Chapter 34, page 180. Valeant Pharmaceutical, IFRS vs GAP accounting standards, audit numbers rigged.

Trick #26 for Farming Humans is printing infinite money to exchange for finite goods…"let me handle that for you." Chapter 35, page 184.

Trick #27 for Farming Humans is public servants spying on the public, and not on the public servants. Chapter 36, page 188.

Trick #28 for Farming Humans is creating a guaranteed maximum income…without having to work for it. Rentier, Banks, etc. Chapter 37, page 190. Jamie Dimon image pg 220, $25 Billion bailout.

Trick #29 for Farming Humans is the bait and switch of promising trust, and then selling out that trust to someone else. Fraudulent advisors and politicians… Chapter 40, page 203.

Trick #30 for Farming Humans is the political bait and switch, Chapter 41, page 208. Breach of Trust, resale of trust.

Post script, Sept 27, 2020

The following study from the Rand Corporation found it's way into my final (hopefully) edit-Version 13 of Farming Humans. It reveals calculations on the cost to society for acts which this book claims to be corrupt or criminal acts upon the public interest, by public officials.

There are links below to two articles, as well as the link to the Rand study itself. I am satisfied that they have done a better job of calculating costs than I could.

It puts into better perspective, the harm done by organized professionals acting in concert, to self-enrich at great expense to the public. Farming Humans is an attempt to show a few of the corrupt acts that allowed society to be cheated by amounts stated in the Rand analysis.

"The true cost of income inequality: $2.5 trillion every year." Each year, $2.5 trillion — yes, trillion with a "T" — has been redistributed from the bottom 90% of Americans to the wealthiest 1 % of all Americans."

https://www.businessinsider.com/wealthiest-1-percent-stole-50-trillion-working-americans-what-means-2020-9

"Economic inequality costs the average working person $42,000 annually"

https://thehill.com/opinion/finance/517772-economic-inequality-costs-the-average-working-person-42000-annually

"From 1975 to 2018, the difference between the aggregate taxable income for those below the 90th percentile and the equitable growth counterfactual totals $47 trillion."

https://www.rand.org/pubs/working_papers/WRA516-1.html

This research was funded by the Fair Work Center and conducted by RAND Education and Labor. This working paper is under review with a scholarly journal; although most RAND working papers are not subject to

About the Author

Larry Elford worked inside Canadian investment dealers for two decades. He saw how high status persons and corporate entities were not subject to the same application of rules or laws as others. Higher status entities were able to "police themselves" or retain their own regulators to "police" their business activities.

He learned how status plus this ability to "self regulate", allowed the growth of corrupt practices, without having to worry that a policeman would come to the office door. Self-regulation also granted the privilege of being able to quietly purchase "exemption" from laws, to further enable corrupt practices without public knowledge or consequences.

Not willing to be an accomplice to harming the public, he spoke out as instructed by codes of conduct and ethics. Those calls for ethics were not welcomed and he felt forced to leave the industry.

He released a documentary film in 2009, titled "Breach of Trust, the Unique Violence of White Collar Crime", after becoming aware of the suicide of an investment industry whistleblower. This person was bullied to his death by industry lawyers and those who used the courts as a mechanism to "hush" persons who spoke about abusive practices.

He gradually learned more about unwritten "codes of silence", which usually received priority over written codes of ethics. The truth teller is most often drummed out of the business, rather than being thanked for the honesty and protection of the firm's reputation.

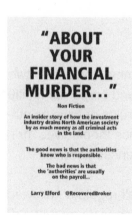

"ABOUT YOUR FINANCIAL MURDER..."

Non Fiction

An insider story of how the investment industry drains North American society by as much money as all criminal acts in the land.

The good news is that the authorities know who is responsible.

The bad news is that the 'authorities' are usually on the payroll...

Larry Elford @RecoveredBroker

The "Unique Violence" he learned about white collar crime is that there is little or no repercussion, accountability, or punishment for the white collar crimes of respectable entities. Mere "tenths" of pennies are spent to police high status economic crime, compared to the dollars spent to police the public at large. These crimes thus become systemic profit-centers which can secretly harvest or drain society by as much money as all other crime in the country, combined.

After testifying in four legislative financial and justice committee inquiries as an industry expert, he learned about the political tentacles which also connect and invisibly protect those greatest crimes upon society.

He has now completed two books, the first on how investment dealers "fee-farm" over half of the life savings of many clients, and this second book about conditions which allow quiet professional corruption to remain hidden from the public, and ignored by authorities.

What drives me? (in the authors words)

Lethbridge Herald @ @Leth_Herald · Nov 9
Financial industry has grip on political system, @SACPA told - @DMabellHerald reports w/ @IMartensHerald photo
lethbridgeherald.com/news/lethbridg …
#yql

I hope to have an impact upon the #1 cause of disability, disease, and stress in society today. I believe I have some unique perspectives on this from my experience.

For example, the #1 cause of disability, disease, and stress is fear of economic uncertainty.

In my experience, the #1 cause of fear of economic uncertainty, is unfairness between those who are protected and enriched within the "lifeboats" of certain professions, corporations or institutions, and those who are not so protected.

There are different levels of protection by the law, and immunity from having to adhere to the law, depending upon the wealth, power or status of those involved. Justice systems simply do not often "look upwards" to investigate and prosecute those of great wealth, power and status.

These rigged systems of governance, finance, justice etc, cause unfairness, injustice, and repeal the laws of poverty for a few very lucky people, and repeals the chances of prosperity for billions of others. A small few win by corruption, while the rest of society must lose by default. This is a broken system.

The unfairness of rigged and/or broken systems, causes imbalances sufficient to destroy entire societies. Societies can literally shake themselves apart with the human vibration of living in an unjust, unfair world.

At time of writing this, I am the chairperson of the volunteer Canadian Justice Review Board of Canada, working to better understand one of societies most valuable social systems, the justice system.

A few years back I held private and commercial helicopter ratings for fun, learning and recreation, but that was another lifetime.